NOBODY LEFT OUT

JESUS MEETS THE MESSES

A 40-DAY DEVOTIONAL FOR
MESSY, BROKEN PEOPLE (LIKE ME!)

Edited by Emily Lupfer

Scriptures are italicized and are taken from the following versions of the Bible:

THE HOLY BIBLE, NEW INTERNATIONAL VERSION®, NIV® Copyright © 1973, 1978, 1984, 2011 by Biblica, Inc.® Used by permission. All rights reserved worldwide.

The Holy Bible, New Living Translation (NLT), copyright © 1996, 2004, 2015 by Tyndale House Foundation. Used by permission of Tyndale House Publishers, Inc., Carol Stream, Illinois 60188. All rights reserved.

THE MESSAGE (MSG), copyright © 1993, 2002, 2018 by Eugene H. Peterson. Used by permission of NavPress. All rights reserved. Represented by Tyndale House Publishers, Inc

Publishing services provided by **Archangel Ink**

Paperback ISBN: 979-8-6999-8864-8
Hardback ISBN: 978-1-7379973-0-6

To anyone who has ever felt broken, messy, or left out.

May we be reminded that Jesus came for people like us.

Contents

Introduction:
Jesus Meets The Messes

A lonely thief.

An unwelcome dinner guest.

A death-row criminal facing his final hours on earth.

What do all of these people have in common? (I promise this isn't the beginning of a bad joke...)

They all faced the messiness of life. Some made the mess themselves. Some were thrown headfirst into a mess through no fault of their own. But they all felt left out in some way.

And then, one day, something changed. It wasn't that they suddenly became *un*messy. Their lives weren't magically made perfect. But through different circumstances, each one came face to face with Jesus. He invited them to be part of God's story. He didn't leave them out.

Over the next 40 days, we're going to look at eight encounters Jesus had with these messy, broken people. Their stories are documented for us in the Bible, along with hundreds of other messy stories.

And that's why I love the Bible. It's so wonderfully messy.

When you open its grimy pages, you won't find a collection of heroes to emulate. Instead, you'll find flawed people who look a lot like you and me. People who struggle to make it through their day. People who get it wrong more than they get it right. People who stumble, fumble, and fail. People who have been overlooked and feel forgotten.

But you'll also find a God whose love is big enough for everyone. A God who includes people, no matter how big of a mess they've gotten themselves into. And let me tell you—as someone who gets into a lot of messes, that gives me hope!

When Jesus walked this earth, he spent time with the messes. Of course, he got pushback for it. The "perfect people" of the world were embarrassed by the company Jesus kept. But one night, while at a raucous dinner party, Jesus explained why he came:

Later, Matthew invited Jesus and his disciples to his home as dinner guests, along with many tax collectors and other disreputable sinners. But when the Pharisees saw this, they asked his disciples, "Why does your teacher eat with such scum?"

When Jesus heard this, he said, "Healthy people don't need a doctor—sick people do." Then he added, "Now go and learn the meaning of this Scripture: 'I want you to show mercy, not offer sacrifices.' For I have come to call not those who think they are righteous, but those who know they are sinners." (Matthew 9:10–13, NLT)

As we look at eight different encounters Jesus had with messy, broken people, I hope you will see reflections of yourself in each story. As Jesus meets them in their messes, I pray you will know he is with you in yours.

Let these stories be a sweet reminder that God doesn't want anyone left out.

And that includes you!

Michael Murray

How To Use This Book

You can use this book in whatever way is most helpful to you. (If you feel like reading it in one sitting, go for it!)

If you are planning to use this book as a daily devotional tool, I want to give you some tips on how to make the most of it.

(By the way, the word *devotional* is simply a fancy, "churchy" word for a brief piece of writing, usually reflecting on a passage found in Scripture.)

In this book, we're going to look at eight encounters Jesus had with people. You can think of these encounters as eight different "scenes" or short stories from Jesus' life.

We'll spend five days looking at each encounter for a total of 40 devotionals. You could approach the reading in one of two ways:

1. You could read one devotional per day for 40 days straight. This is a great way to build a daily habit of reading the Bible.

2. You could spread the reading out over eight weeks, devoting one week to each encounter. To do this, you would read one devotional Monday–Friday and take the weekends off. (Or use the weekends to catch up on any missed days!)

Again, there's no right or wrong way to approach this. Do whatever works best for you. And if you miss a day of reading, don't stress or get discouraged! Just pick back up the next day. We don't earn "God Points" by reading the Bible every day. As we'll see from these stories, there's nothing we can do to make God love us any more than he already does. Our goal is just to get to know our friend Jesus better!

Here are a few more reading tips...

* In the introduction page for each encounter, I'll give the Scripture reference for where you can find that story in the Bible. I suggest taking a few minutes to read the full passage before starting on the devotionals. Over the five days, we'll walk through the story chronologically, looking at it from all sides and perspectives. But it will be helpful to get a big-picture view of the story before diving in!

* On some days, there will be a "supporting" passage of Scripture to read. These verses will provide more context for the story we are exploring. I recommend reading the supporting passage before reading the day's devotional.

* If you're looking for a quick, easy way to access the Bible, consider downloading the YouVersion Bible App. Another great resource is *BibleGateway.com*.

* There are many different Bible translations. I don't believe any single translation is the "best"—they all convey God's truth. (One of my favorite things to do is look at the same verse in multiple translations. It helps me understand it from a different perspective and gain new insight!) Throughout this book, I primarily quote from the New International Version (NIV), the New Living Translation (NLT), and The Message (MSG). When reading the daily verses, feel free to use your preferred version. (You can even decide to go old school and whip out the King James Version. Thou art awesome!)

* At the end of each devotional, I've included some questions to ponder. As with everything in this book, use them in whatever way is most helpful to you. My hope is they will give you

something to reflect on throughout the day. You may connect with some deeper than others.

* Each day's reading should take about 10–15 minutes to complete (including reading the Bible verses). Here's my biggest piece of advice: Don't view reading the Bible as a chore. If you get through this devotional in 40 days, that's great. But you know what? If it takes you 40 years, that's okay, too! If it helps to schedule the reading at the same time every day, then do it. But if you're not a morning person, don't feel obligated to read it at five in the morning. (At least get some coffee in you first!) Maybe lunch is a better time for you to read. Or right before bed. Do whatever works best for you.

Okay, that's it for the housekeeping. Let's get on to the fun stuff and meet our first mess!

Encounter I:
Jesus Meets The Lonely Thief

Zacchaeus was a man who traded relationships for fortune. He turned his back on his heritage to line his pockets with wealth stolen from his neighbors.

But Zacchaeus—like all of us—had his reasons for doing what he did. There was more going on with Zacchaeus under the surface: a deep pain no one knew about.

Then one day, Jesus waltzed into town.
And everything changed.

* * *

You can find the story of the Lonely Thief in **Luke 19:1-10**. Take a few minutes to read it, and then we'll jump in!

- Day 1 -
There Is No One Like Jesus

Today's Bible Reading: Luke 19:1-10

I've been to Malawi, Africa four times to work alongside a wonderful organization called Children of the Nations (COTN). Although the very thought of stepping aboard a plane fills me with dread, I always look forward to spending time with my friends there. I also look forward to the singing. In Malawi, it's a guarantee that at some point during the day, you're going to burst into joyful song (accompanied by dancing, of course). My favorite song sung in the Malawian language of Chichewa is called "Palibe Ofana Ndi Yesu." Translated into English, it means "There is No One Like Jesus." Here are the words:

There's no one, there's no one like Jesus
There's no one, there's no one like Jesus

I wandered
I wandered everywhere
I turned around everywhere
I searched everywhere
And still, I haven't found anyone like Jesus

I've been singing that song for years, appreciating the lyrics but never giving them much thought. But then one morning on my most recent trip to Malawi, the lyrics stopped me right in my tracks. As we stood there singing along with the COTN staff, I became overwhelmed by the truth of those simple words. When you look at the life of Jesus and see the invitation he offered to others—how he loved and included all people—it's hard to find anyone else that compares to him.

That's why we're going to spend the next 40 days looking at eight stories of people who crossed paths with Jesus. Some thought they had life all figured out. Others were at the end of their rope, desperately trying to find any scrap of hope they could cling to. Their stories have very little in common except for this: After meeting Jesus, they all realized there was no one like him.

We'll start things off by looking at one of my favorite stories in the Bible: the story of Zacchaeus. Take some time today to read his story. Zacchaeus was a con man and a traitor to his own people. I'm sure you could make a Netflix original series chronicling all of his shady dealings (I can just see it... Don't miss *Sneaky Zach*, available to stream this spring!). And yet, when Jesus came to town, Zacchaeus zipped up a tree to get a better look at him. Why? Maybe he'd heard the stories. Stories that there was no one like this strange man called Jesus.

💬 Questions to Ponder:

Why do you think Zacchaeus was so eager to see Jesus?

What stories have you heard about Jesus?

- Day 2 -
The Lonely Thief

Today's Bible Reading: Luke 19:1-10 (focus on verses 1-4)
Supporting Passage: Luke 18:35-43

The Bible doesn't give us a lot of details about Zacchaeus, but it does provide us with some important clues into the kind of man he was. The name *Zacchaeus* means "pure" or "clean" in Hebrew. Despite this, Zacchaeus created some messes for himself.

Zacchaeus was Jewish, but he took a job with the Roman government as a tax collector (and a chief tax collector, no less). This was a slap in the face to his own people. As much as we make jokes about "the taxman" today, the system was much more twisted in ancient Rome. The government gave Zacchaeus the power to tax the Jews as much as he wanted. Once "Uncle Caesar" collected his cut, Zacchaeus was free to pocket the rest. Zacchaeus got rich by cheating his own family.

There is another bit of information about Zacchaeus that Luke provides: He was a short man. As I ponder that detail, it makes me wonder if Zacchaeus had some kind of disability. Did he have some sort of deformity that people mocked? There is a children's song about Zacchaeus that goes, *Zacchaeus was a wee little man, and a wee little man was he.* That's humiliating, isn't it? Even Christians can't help pointing out his physical flaw.

I have a disability called cerebral palsy. I've sprinkled in a few stories throughout this book about how it has affected my life. Growing up,

I felt lonely around my peers at times. It wasn't that they pointed, laughed, and made fun of me. Some days I just felt left out. Maybe Zacchaeus did, too. I wonder if he already felt like an outcast before he took the tax collector job. Perhaps he thought, "Okay. If this is how these people are going to treat me, let's see how they like it when I start taking their money!"

I don't think money fulfilled Zacchaeus the way he thought it would. Our stuff can amuse us for a while, but pretty soon every new toy we get becomes ordinary. It's not that we stop using our things; they just become second nature to us. I don't appreciate having an iPad the way I did the week I first got it. These days, I just get annoyed when it's not working correctly.

Zacchaeus wanted something more, but he didn't quite know what. And then Jesus strolled into town. Jesus healed a blind man right before he entered Jericho, and it attracted a lot of attention. (That's our supporting passage for today, and it's worth reading. Everyone was telling the blind man to shut up, but he was too desperate to let Jesus pass by without noticing him!) Maybe Zacchaeus heard rumors about this miracle and wanted to get a glimpse of who this Jesus guy was.

And so Zacchaeus climbed a tree, an act that would have been humiliating for a grown man. But Zacchaeus was used to being humiliated. It appears Zacchaeus was seeking Jesus. But, as we'll see tomorrow, it was Jesus who was seeking him.

 Questions to Ponder:

When have you felt like an outcast?

What part of Zacchaeus's story do you relate to the most?

- Day 3 -
When Jesus Smiles

Today's Bible Reading: Luke 19:1-10 (focus on verses 5-6)
Supporting Passage: Luke 15:11-32

Luke tells us that Jesus was passing through Jericho. That means he was headed somewhere else. He was on his way to Jerusalem to celebrate Passover with his disciples. By the end of the week he would be arrested, tried, and crucified. Jesus was literally carrying the weight of the world on his shoulders, and yet he stopped everything to see Zacchaeus.

Picture this scene: people crowd the streets of Jericho, pushing and pulling their way to Jesus. Maybe a few elbows are thrown! I'm sure the disciples are in crowd control mode, but Jesus remains calm. There is someone he needs to see while he happens to be in town—someone who has been on his mind for a long time.

When Jesus reaches the tree Zacchaeus is hiding in, he stops. Then, he looks up at Zacchaeus and smiles at him. Okay, the Bible doesn't tell us that Jesus smiled. But trust me, I know he did. Look at what Jesus calls up to Zacchaeus:

When Jesus reached the spot, he looked up and said to him, "Zacchaeus, come down immediately. I must stay at your house today." (Luke 19:5, NIV)

Look at the joy in Jesus' words! "Zacchaeus, come on down! We need to hang out today. I'm clearing my calendar for you, buddy!"

Yes, Jesus smiled at Zacchaeus. A big, huge, welcoming smile. Jesus is joyful when he finds Zacchaeus in that tree. And the joy is contagious. Luke tells us that Zacchaeus came down and welcomed Jesus gladly. But that doesn't quite capture the excitement. The Message version puts it this way:

Zacchaeus scrambled out of the tree, hardly believing his good luck, delighted to take Jesus home with him. (Luke 19:6, MSG)

There is an urgency in Zacchaeus. He needs to be with Jesus. A few chapters before this happens, Jesus tells the story of the Prodigal Son. Now he's living it out for all to see. The story of Zacchaeus is the real-life Prodigal Son story. Jesus is the father, welcoming the rebellious younger brother home with open arms. The past is the past. Regret has given way to celebration. Zacchaeus's guilt and shame seem to melt away when Jesus finds him.

Author J. Ellsworth Kalas puts it like this:

There's nothing the divine Heart wants so much as to have the whole family come home, to have all the lost sheep, lost coins, and lost sons and daughters found.[1]

Do you think Jesus would ever smile at you? Sometimes I think he's too disappointed in me to smile. But that's a lie. Even when we're a mess, Jesus smiles at us, calls us by name, and invites us to come home.

💬 Questions to Ponder:

Knowing what you know of Zacchaeus's story, why do you think he was so happy when Jesus called him down?

How will you respond when Jesus smiles at you?

---

1   Kalas, J. Ellsworth. *Parables from the Back Side: Bible Stories with a Twist.* Nashville, TN: Abingdon Press, 1992.

- Day 4 -
Measuring Sticks

Today's Bible Reading: Luke 19:1-10 (focus on verse 7)

Yesterday I shared that Jesus smiled when he called up to Zacchaeus in the tree. I believe this because of the joy in Jesus' words. But there is another clue, too: the way the crowd reacts when they see Jesus offer an invitation to Zacchaeus.

All the people saw this and began to mutter, "He has gone to be the guest of a sinner." (Luke 19:7, NIV)

The NLT version of the Bible uses the term "notorious sinner," which I find pretty funny. He was the Notorious Zachy, and it offended the good people in the neighborhood that Jesus would choose to share a meal with him. They were jealous. If Jesus was going over to Zacchaeus's house, it meant they were going to eat together. Sharing a meal had significant relational implications in the ancient world. They were so upset they couldn't even call Zacchaeus by name (yet, ironically, it was the first word out of Jesus' mouth). All they could manage to mutter was the word "sinner."

Why do you think that is?

I think the people of Jericho used Zacchaeus as a measuring stick, and I mean that both literally and metaphorically. As I alluded to a couple of days ago, Zacchaeus may have had a physical disability. If not a disability, he at least looked different enough for people to take notice. He was an easy mark to compare yourself to and come out ahead.

And morally speaking, it didn't matter what your sin was—Zacchaeus had you beat. I can just hear the town chatter: *"Yes, yes, I know I lost my temper and said some unkind things today. But at least I'm not as bad as that lying, cheating, funny-looking thief Zacchaeus. He's the real sinner!"*

When I read Bible stories, I typically put myself in the shoes of the main character. I'm David, working up the courage to face Goliath. I'm Peter, reaching out to Jesus as I'm sinking in the sea. I'm even Zacchaeus, the outcast whom Jesus chooses to invite over for dinner. But I think it's important to approach a Bible story from the point of view of every character. The stories in the Bible are not simple fairy tales where there are clear "good guys" and "bad guys." It's a book full of messy humans. That's what makes it so fascinating.

The truth is, I'm more like the people of Jericho than I realize. I compare myself to others to make myself feel better. And on the flip side, when I see someone who I perceive as "better" than me, I compare myself and feel like a failure. But Jesus came for everyone. His love isn't finite. He loved every person in that town as much as he loved Zacchaeus. We don't have to compare ourselves to others because God doesn't want anyone left out.

💬 Questions to Ponder:

When are you most tempted to use someone as a "measuring stick" of comparison?

Is there anyone you have left out or written off because you thought they were a lost cause? How can you take one step toward them in love?

- Day 5 -
Stumbling Saints

Today's Bible Reading: Luke 19:1-10 (focus on verses 8-10)

I can't believe it's almost time to say goodbye to our friend Zacchaeus. There is so much I love about his story. But before we can bid him farewell, we need to look at how his life changed the day he met Jesus.

Even as the crowd is mocking Zacchaeus for being a "sinner," he is being transformed. He boldly proclaimed to Jesus:

Here and now I give half of my possessions to the poor, and if I have cheated anybody out of anything [which he knows he has!], *I will pay back four times the amount.* (Luke 19:8, NIV)

That number is significant. According to Israelite law, if you stole something you had to pay back the amount taken plus 20% on top of it. In the most extreme cases, however, the maximum penalty was paying back 400% of the amount. Zacchaeus, now realizing how broken and messy he is, happily sentences himself to the severest punishment. No one can deny that Zacchaeus was a changed man after meeting Jesus. But that's where things get complicated for Zacchaeus—and all of us.

I once heard it said that Zacchaeus was "the man who went up a tree a sinner and came down a saint." That sounds nice, and if it's true, it ties everything together with a neat little bow. But it would also continue making Zacchaeus a measuring stick for all who read his story. Do we measure up to Zacchaeus? Have our lives been transformed in such a radical way?

The truth is, we don't know how Zacchaeus's story ended. We never read about him again. I'm not suggesting he didn't make good on his promise. I think from that day forward, Zacchaeus lived life with honesty and integrity. And that's hard to do. Were there days Zacchaeus felt tempted to go back to his old ways? Were there days he messed up? Were there days he flat-out lied and cheated again? I think so. Why? Because I'm a follower of Jesus, and I mess up every day!

You may think I'm ending the story of Zacchaeus on a bummer note. But recognizing that Zacchaeus still had struggles can bring hope to our own stories. There is a line in the song "Day By Day"[2] by the band Citizens that goes:

My will is changing day by day
I'm not who I was; now I am who I am, a sinner saved
A stumbling saint

I love that term *stumbling saint*. It's a paradox, but one I understand far too well. So maybe Zacchaeus was actually "the man who went up a tree a sinner and came down a stumbling saint." He was found by Jesus and changed by his love and forgiveness. And Jesus would stay by him, even when things got messy again.

Just like he does for all of us stumbling saints.

 Questions to Ponder:

What do you think Zacchaeus's life was like after he met Jesus?

What do you think of the term *stumbling saint*? Does it describe you?

What is one thing you've learned about Jesus from the story of the Lonely Thief?

---

2   Citizens. *Day by Day. A Mirror Dimly*. Brian Eichelberger, 2016.

Encounter II:
Jesus Meets The Know-It-All

At first glance, a person like Nathanael may seem out of place in a book about messes. He was a smart young man who had life all figured out.

Nathanael carried around a healthy dose of skepticism wherever he went. He longed for the Messiah like any good Israelite in his day—and he knew it couldn't possibly be someone like Jesus.

An argument wasn't going to convince Nathanael. But maybe an inside joke from Jesus would.

* * *

You can find the story of The Know-It-All in **John 1:35-51**. Take a few minutes to read it, and then we'll jump in!

- Day 6 -
Come, See, And Follow

Today's Bible Reading: John 1:35-51

Our second encounter is between Jesus and a young man named Nathanael. Although Nathanael was skeptical of Jesus at first, he would soon become one of Jesus' disciples. But before we dive into Nathanael's story, I want to spend today looking at who these disciples were and how Jesus chose them.

The disciples were 12 men who lived and worked alongside Jesus. He was their teacher, mentor, and friend. And when it came time for Jesus to leave this world, he gave them the job of spreading his message "to the ends of the earth" (Acts 1:8). What a responsibility! Jesus only had three years to spend with his disciples, and it was going to be a tough ride. You would think he'd make things a *little easier* on himself by picking the best and brightest of the pack. You know—young men with raw talent who he could mold into greatness. But Jesus rarely took the easy route.

If Jesus had read a book or two about leadership, he might have selected a more qualified bunch. Instead, Jesus built a team of misfits, losers, and eccentrics. It was like the Bad News Bears.

He chose Matthew, a tax collector. (We all know what people thought of tax collectors from Zacchaeus's story.) He chose Peter, a passionate man but also a loose cannon with no filter. He chose Thomas, a pessimist who loved to point out the worst outcome in any situation. He chose Judas, a schemer who Jesus knew would sell him out for a quick payday. And he chose Nathanael, a know-it-all kid who thought he had life figured out. These are not the kind of people you'd want on a team. But Jesus wanted them.

What's also interesting is *how* Jesus recruited this team. Right before his interaction with Nathanael, Jesus met two other disciples. When they asked him where he was staying, Jesus responded, "Come, and you will see" (v. 39). And when he met Philip the next day, he simply said, "Follow me" (v. 43).

Christians can put a lot of emphasis on people "making a decision" to believe in Jesus. We want to know, "Do you believe that Jesus is the Son of God who came to die on the cross for your sins?" It's an important question to wrestle with. But Jesus' first words to his disciples weren't "believe in me" or "obey me." Instead, he invited them to come, see, and follow. It's the same invitation Jesus offers to us. The order isn't "believe, then follow"; it's "follow, then believe."

We can follow Jesus even when we're not sure what we believe about him yet.

💬 Questions to Ponder:

Why do you think Jesus chose such a messy group of people to follow him?

If you're a Christian, why did you start following Jesus?

If you're not a Christian, what do you think of Jesus' invitation to "come, see, and follow"?

- Day 7 -
The Eye Roll

Today's Bible Reading: John 1:43-51 (focus on verses 43-46)

In the musical *Les Misérables*, a group of students revolt against the corrupt Paris government. The group is led by Enjolras, a passionate man willing to sacrifice everything to see change. He leads his fellow revolutionaries in the rousing anthem, "Do You Hear The People Sing?"

I imagine someone like Enjolras when I think of Nathanael. Like Enjolras, Nathanael hung out with a group of like-minded young men who dreamed of revolution. Israel was under the thumb of Roman rule, and they longed to be set free. Nathanael and his friends knew God had promised to send Israel a savior. They all had theories on what that savior—the rightful king of Israel—would be like. But when Philip suggested that Jesus from Nazareth was the promised one, Nathanael scoffed.

"Nazareth! Can anything good come from there?" Nathanael asked. (John 1:46, NIV)

Nazareth was a small, backwater district where nothing exciting ever happened. Nathanael quickly dismissed Jesus because he came from "the wrong side of town."

In his book *Encounters with Jesus*, Tim Keller says, "Dismissiveness kills all creativity and problem-solving."[3] How quick are we to shut down a conversation because the other person "just doesn't get it"? Nathanael pounced on Philip's idea that Jesus could be the savior. The Message version of the Bible puts his response this way:

"Nazareth? You've got to be kidding."

That sounds like a reply you might see on a Facebook post!

Keller goes on to say there is one surefire way to tell if you're being dismissive: check for the eye roll. If I'm rolling my eyes at someone, I'm dismissing their ideas—and maybe even dismissing them as a person. That's a dangerous place to be. It means I've shut myself off from learning about them. I can't roll my eyes and show compassion at the same time.

I've seen both Christians and atheists have dismissive attitudes. Christians dismiss atheists for ridiculous ideas like evolution *(because God wouldn't use evolution as a method of creating life!)*. Atheists dismiss Christians for ridiculous ideas like creation *(because evolution wouldn't need God's hand to guide it!)*. Soon, we're all rolling our eyes at each other.

So how do we fight off dismissiveness when we feel it creeping into our lives? One way is to think the best of people! Assume they've thought through their ideas. When someone holds a view that goes against mine, I can either dismiss them or ask them why they hold that opinion. Curiosity invites conversation and builds friendships with people who are different from me.

What if we're on the other end of dismissiveness? What if, like Philip, our ideas are met with a "you've got to be kidding" response? We'll look at the brilliant way Philip dealt with Nathanael's eye roll tomorrow.

---

3   Keller, Timothy. *Encounters with Jesus: Unexpected Answers to Life's Biggest Questions*. New York, NY: Penguin Books, 2013.

💬 Questions to Ponder:

Why do you think Nathanael dismissed Jesus so quickly?

What (or whose) ideas are you most likely to dismiss? How can you invite conversation instead?

- Day 8 -
Win The Argument, Lose The Friend

Today's Bible Reading: John 1:43-51 (focus on verse 46)
Supporting Passage: 1 Peter 3:13-17

Yesterday, we looked at what happened when Philip tried to share the good news of Jesus with his buddy Nathanael. Nathanael rolled his eyes and scoffed, "Nazareth! Can anything good come from there?"

How did Philip respond to this harsh criticism? With three words:

"Come and see."

What a brilliant reply! Philip doesn't get defensive. He doesn't lash out and hit Nathanael with a sarcastic comeback. He doesn't even try to appeal to Nathanael's logic and explain all the reasons why Jesus is the Messiah. Instead, he calmly replies, "Come and see for yourself, and then you can decide."

We can learn a lot from Philip's response. In a sincere effort to "defend my faith," I've often felt pressure to answer every criticism of Christianity. In college I had some friends who would ask me questions like: *How do you know the Bible is true? Do you really believe all that Noah's Ark stuff? What do you think of this weird Old Testament law? Does it seem very loving to you?* I would become flustered, trying to bat away all their objections. I would leave feeling like I lost a debate.

I should have taken the Philip approach and replied, "You know, those are good questions, guys. I don't have all the answers. But here's what Jesus did for me. I think you should take a look at him."

A quick scroll through Facebook will show you how much people love to win arguments. But being "right" doesn't seem to be Philip's primary goal. He wants to introduce his friend to Jesus. He doesn't ask anything of Nathanael other than to come, see, and then draw an opinion.

I'm not saying we shouldn't have intelligent answers to tough questions about God. We *should*. But answers alone rarely satisfy people. And all the answers in the world won't do any good if they're delivered with a condescending attitude. The Apostle Peter reminds us:

[I]f someone asks about your hope as a believer, always be ready to explain it. But do this in a gentle and respectful way. Keep your conscience clear. (1 Peter 3:15–16, NLT)

The best way to explain my hope is to point people to Jesus. But if they roll their eyes at me, my gut reaction is to say something to make them feel as stupid as they've made me feel. (Wow. That's tough to admit in writing!) I may win the argument, but I'll also lose the relationship. I want to be like Philip: "Just come and see." And to Nathanael's credit, he went and saw.

🗨 Questions to Ponder:

If you're a follower of Jesus, have you ever felt pressure to answer every criticism of Christianity? How can you use the "Philip Approach" the next time you're in a situation like that?

If you're not a follower of Jesus, is there one step you can take to "come and see" who Jesus is?

- Day 9 -
Jesus The Jokester

Today's Bible Reading: John 1:43-51 (focus on verses 47-48)

Over the past few days, we've been looking at the exchange between Philip and Nathanael. We've seen Nathanael roll his eyes at the idea that Jesus could be the Messiah. And we've heard Philip's response—a gentle invitation to Nathanael to come see Jesus for himself. Now Jesus and Nathanael come face to face, and Jesus decides to break the ice... *with a joke!*

As Jesus sees Nathanael approaching, he smiles and calls out:

"Here truly is an Israelite in whom there is no deceit." (John 1:47, NIV)

Jesus was making a pun!

The Israelites descended from the line of Abraham, Isaac, and Jacob. The name Jacob means *deceiver*, and boy, did that name fit him well. In the book of Genesis, we see Jacob deceive people over and over again. (The book of Genesis is a very messy book. If you think your family has issues, I encourage you to read it. You'll feel better!) Jacob cheated his brother, deceived his father, and got into a practical joke war with his uncle. He finally met his match when he got into a wrestling bout with God. After the fight, God changed Jacob's name to Israel, which means *struggles with God*.

When Jesus says that Nathanael is "an Israelite in whom there is no deceit," he is using a play on words. He's literally saying, "Here comes the deceiver who doesn't deceive."

Christians are quick to affirm that Jesus was fully God. It can be harder to remember that Jesus was also fully human. We know that there were times when Jesus wept (John 11:35, shortest verse in the Bible!), but there were also times he laughed. There were times he laughed so hard his sides ached, and he couldn't breathe. Imagine that! Jesus wasn't above cracking a joke.

Humor can either tear people down or build bridges between them. All too often, I opt for the former. It's easy to make a quick joke at someone's expense. But Jesus' joke had a purpose. Jesus knew Nathanael was looking for truth, and Jesus affirmed that quality in him. He was saying, *Nathanael! Now here comes a guy who tells it like it is. A real straight-shooter!* Jesus was meeting Nathanael in his skepticism.

I'm glad that when we roll our eyes at Jesus, he gives us grace. Sometimes, that grace comes in the form of a joke. Jesus knew that Nathanael was critical of him, and rather than take offense, he laughed it off. He eased the tension and used the moment to make Nathanael feel known. That's what Jesus does for all of us. He offers us the gift of being fully known by him.

Taken aback by this, Nathanael asks, "How do you know me?"

He'll soon find out that Jesus knows him better than anyone.

🗨 Questions to Ponder:

Which do you have a harder time believing or imagining: that Jesus was "fully God" or "fully human"?

Jesus can meet us anywhere—in skepticism, doubt, fear, anger, sadness, and joy. Where do you need Jesus to meet you today?

- Day 10 -
Known By Jesus

Today's Bible Reading: John 1:43-51 (focus on verses 48-51)

Over the past five days, we've spent some time with our skeptical friend Nathanael. Although he rolled his eyes at Jesus, he was willing to come and see what all the fuss was about. And when they came face to face, Jesus eased the tension by telling a joke that complimented Nathanael. Surprised by this, Nathanael asked, "How do you know me?"

Jesus' response to this question seems very odd at first glance. This is what he said:

Jesus answered, "I saw you while you were still under the fig tree before Philip called you." (John 1:48, NIV)

Huh? Fig tree? When I first read that, I thought I missed something. I went back through the passage to see if I skipped the part about Nathanael being under the fig tree. Nope. There's no mention of it. So... *what was Nathanael doing under the fig tree?* No one knows! It was a private moment between him and Jesus.

The fig tree was a place of prayer for young Israelites like Nathanael. Many scholars speculate that Nathanael was praying for the coming Messiah. So when Jesus says that he saw him under the fig tree, Nathanael connects that Jesus is the one he's been praying for. That makes sense, but it's just a guess. Prayer is something deeply personal, and we don't get the details of other people's prayer lives.

Nathanael could have been talking to God about anything. He could have been unleashing his anger, expressing his fears, or weeping in sadness. Whatever he was doing, Jesus saw him. And when Nathanael heard this, it filled him with so much wonder that he declared:

"Rabbi, you are the Son of God; you are the king of Israel." (John 1:49, NIV)

Several years ago, there was a small park near my house I would visit. I would sit on the swing by myself and talk to God about all the things I was angry about, worried about, and sad about. That swing was my fig tree. And looking back now, I can see I wasn't alone. I imagine Jesus saying to me, all these years later, "Michael, I saw you while you were still on the swing."

What turns a skeptic into a believer? Being known by Jesus. An argument didn't convince Nathanael. But when he found out that Jesus saw him in his most vulnerable moment, it brought him to his knees. And Jesus smiled and said, *Nathanael, we're just getting started. Don't be so easily impressed. You won't believe the things I have in store for you.*

The story of Nathanael is a reminder that Jesus sees us in our pain and brokenness. He sees us in the places of our doubt, anger, and deepest longings. Jesus sees us because he doesn't want anyone left out.

💬 Questions to Ponder:

Why do you think Nathanael was so surprised that Jesus saw him under the fig tree?

Where is your "fig tree"—the place you go to express all your hidden secrets, doubts, and fears? How does it feel to know Jesus is with you in that place?

What is one thing you've learned about Jesus from the story of The Know-It-All?

Encounter III:
Jesus Meets The Unwelcome Dinner Guest

The clinking of silverware. Voices around the table. An important man is throwing a dinner party, and Jesus is the guest of honor.

Then she enters the room. Everyone knows this woman is a major mess. And now she's causing a scene by weeping at Jesus' feet.

What will Jesus do now that this unwelcome dinner guest has shown up? He does what any life of the party would do. He tells a story.

* * *

You can find the story of The Unwelcome Dinner Guest in **Luke 7:36-50**. Take a few minutes to read it, and then we'll jump in!

- Day 11 -
Jesus & Women

Today's Bible Reading: Luke 7:36-50
Supporting Passage: Matthew 28:1-10

For our next few encounters, we're going to look at some of the inter-actions Jesus had with women. But before we begin, I want to give a disclaimer.

I am writing this devotional from a male perspective. As a man, I think it's important to see the way Jesus treated women while he walked this earth. I can learn a lot from his example. Over the past few years, our society has made some progress in reconciling how we've treated women. We still have a long way to go, and I believe the first step is listening. The sad irony for Christian men is that we've had the example of Jesus to look to this whole time. (And the good news is, we still do!) As I write about the interactions Jesus had with women, I want humility to guide me. I am open to correction.

Jesus was a fierce defender of women in a culture that devalued them. In the ancient world, women had very few legal rights, and they were often exploited by men in power (something we still see today). There are several stories—including the one we're looking at this week—where "religious" men tried to use women as a tool against Jesus. But Jesus refused to allow them to use women as a pawn in their game. Lee Anna Starr writes:

Of all founders of religions and religious sects, Jesus stands alone as the one who did

not discriminate in some way against women. By word or deed he never encouraged
the disparagement of a woman.[4]

Beyond not discriminating against women, Jesus invited and included them in his ministry. Women were among Jesus' most faithful followers. He taught them and respected their intelligence. (There was no mansplaining from Jesus!) And after the resurrection, Jesus appeared to "Mary Magdalene and the other Mary" (Matthew 28:1). Jesus gave these two women the awesome responsibility of telling the disciples he was alive! Clearly, Jesus saw women as a vital part of spreading the good news.

This week, we'll be looking at the story of a woman who crashed a dinner party. We don't know her name, but I'm calling her The Unwelcome Dinner Guest because she made the host of the party very uncomfortable. Through her story, Jesus teaches us an extraordinary lesson about the ways we perceive our own brokenness.

💬 Questions to Ponder:

In what ways were Jesus' attitudes toward women counter-cultural?

Take some time today to read Luke 7:36–50. What are some things that stand out to you? What are some things you learned from the story?

---

4   Starr, Lee Anna. *The Bible Status of Woman*. Zarephath, N.J.: Pillar of Fire, 1955.

- Day 12 -
A Willingness To Be Broken

Today's Bible Reading: Luke 7:36-50 (focus on verses 36-38)

Luke is my favorite gospel writer. All four gospels show Jesus' compassion for people, but Luke seems to relish in telling stories about the forgotten and the rejected—people who are shunned by society. People like the Unwelcome Dinner Guest, who risked public shame to get to the feet of Jesus.

Luke tells us that Jesus was having dinner with a Pharisee named Simon. In that culture, outsiders were permitted to drop in on dinner parties to listen to what the "important" people had to say. It's a bit odd; imagine showing up to dinner at the royal palace. You wouldn't get a plate, but you'd be free to listen in on the royal chatter! (I.e., all the cute things little Prince Louie did today.)

While the meal was in progress, a woman "who lived a sinful life" (v. 37) came into the house and started weeping at the feet of Jesus. I've read several commentaries that try to pinpoint what her specific sins might have been. We love guessing the sins of other people, don't we? Instead of trying to figure out what *her* sins were, my time might be better spent reflecting on *my own* sinful life.

I can't imagine how much courage it took for her to make such a public display of affection toward Jesus. She wasn't quietly weeping in the corner. She caused a scene! Think of how many tears it must take to drench feet. She was violently sobbing right in front of men who had no compassion for her at all. And when the tears ran out, she took her perfume—maybe the only thing of value she owned—and poured it on Jesus' feet.

What drove her to the feet of Jesus? Was she overwhelmed with sorrow for the life she'd been leading? Was her spirit completely broken by the abuse she endured from others? Did she hear rumors that there was someone in town who shows kindness and compassion to outcasts? Or had Jesus forgiven her sometime earlier, and she came back to express the gratitude in her heart?

It could be any of those things. All I know is, I have a lot to learn from this woman. I admire her willingness to be broken. Her willingness to express sorrow. Her vulnerability to go to Jesus, even when the rest of the world is glaring at her. I wish I were like that.

The Unwelcome Dinner Guest dared to enter that house because she knew she was welcomed by Jesus. His opinion was the only one that mattered. She was free to lay all of her guilt, shame, disappointments, and burdens at his feet. Just like Jesus invites us all to do.

🗨 Questions to Ponder:

What are some things that keep you from going to Jesus?

What burdens, worries, or sins do you want to lay at the feet of Jesus? Take a few minutes to do that today.

- Day 13 -
Jesus RSVPs "Yes" To Every Evite

Today's Bible Reading: Luke 7:36-50 (focus on verse 39)

Over the past few days, we've been looking at the story of a woman who crashed a dinner party so that she could get to Jesus. Today, I want to shift our attention to the host of the party—a Pharisee named Simon.

Pharisees get a bad rap in the New Testament. Whenever Jesus got angry, it was usually because of something a Pharisee said or did. But what exactly is a Pharisee? Here's one definition (I found it on Google, so we know it's true):

A member of an ancient Jewish sect, distinguished by strict observance of the traditional and written law, and commonly held to have pretensions to superior sanctity.[5]

I find that last part interesting: "and commonly held to have pretensions to superior sanctity."

It wasn't always like that. Pharisees had a high and noble calling. It was their job to help people grow closer to God. But somewhere along the line, they started judging people rather than loving them. All of their self-made laws created a chasm between them and their flock. Only they were good enough to get to God.

---

5   "Pharisee: Definition of Pharisee by Oxford Dictionary on Lexico.com Also Meaning of Pharisee." Lexico Dictionaries | English. Lexico Dictionaries. https://www.lexico.com/en/definition/pharisee.

And yet, here was Jesus, dining at the home of a Pharisee. The Pharisees would often grumble when Jesus ate with "sinners" (tax collectors, prostitutes, etc.). But I wonder—did those same sinners ever complain when Jesus dined with Pharisees? Did they scratch their heads and say, "Hey, wait, I thought that was *our* guy…"

Can you imagine if a Hollywood celebrity had dinner with the highest-ranking Republican in Congress on Monday and then on Tuesday ate lunch with their Democratic counterpart? People would be confused. The celebrity would be accused of sending mixed messages or not taking a stand for one side or the other. But you can't box in Jesus. He RSVPs "yes" to every evite because he knows that both sinners and Pharisees need his grace.

When Simon saw the woman start to weep at Jesus' feet, he said to himself:

If this man were a prophet, he would know who is touching him and what kind of woman she is—that she is a sinner. (v. 39, NIV)

Simon is making three wrong assumptions with that statement:

1. Simon is assuming Jesus doesn't know who this woman is. *(Jesus knows everything about her story.)*

2. Simon is assuming the woman can't get close to God. *(She can.)*

3. Simon is assuming he's a better person than the woman. *(He's not.)*

If I were Jesus, I would have gotten up and walked right out of that house. But Jesus stays. He loves Simon so much that he wants to teach him a profound lesson in forgiveness. And so, rather than getting upset, Jesus did something that fit in well at a dinner party: He told a story.

💬 Questions to Ponder:

Which character do you relate to more—The Unwelcome Dinner Guest or Simon?

It can be so easy to judge people who are judging others. How can we break the "Pharisee Cycle" and love them instead?

- Day 14 -
A Tale Of Two Debtors

Today's Bible Reading: Luke 7:36-50 (focus on verses 39-43)

If I've learned anything from financial planner Dave Ramsey, it's that there's no such thing as "good debt." But the only way to get out of debt is to admit you have debt. (Then you can get that debt snowball rolling!)

After Simon begins judging the woman at Jesus' feet, Jesus launches into a simple parable. Two people were in debt. One for a lot of money, the other for a little. Neither had the money to pay the banker back, so he canceled both their debts. *(That's how you can tell Jesus made up the story. No banker would ever do that in real life!)*

After telling the story, Jesus asks Simon, "Now which of them will love [the banker] more?"

Simon replies (maybe with an eye roll), "I suppose the one who had the bigger debt forgiven."

Jesus was offering Simon a new perspective with this story. Both people were in debt. One was just able to manage it a little better. One didn't feel the creditors breathing down his neck as closely as the other did. One was able to say, "Well, yeah, I have a little debt, but it's not a big deal. I still have control over my life." But he was still in debt and still in need of forgiveness.

Tenth-grade geometry was my absolute worst subject. I had no clue what was going on during class most of the time. I thought geometry would be easy since I know all my shapes, but it was a nightmare. Sorry, now I'm going on a tangent. *(Geometry joke!)*

My only saving grace was that my teacher was kind. On the day of a big test one afternoon, he announced that we could take our test in groups. What?! I was so happy I could have kissed the man. I happened to sit by the three smartest guys in class, so I passed the test with flying colors through no effort of my own.

I was fully aware of my need for a math savior. And I knew that the group test was a gift of grace from the teacher. But how often do I go through life thinking my debt to God is no big deal? How often do I act like Simon—pointing my finger at someone who has a "bigger debt" than me?

The woman at Jesus' feet wasn't more of a sinner than Simon. She was just more aware of her need. And that allowed her to experience Jesus' grace in a more significant way. Theologian Matthew Henry puts it like this:

None can truly perceive how precious Christ is, and the glory of the gospel, except the broken-hearted.[6]

 Questions to Ponder:

What do you think was the point of the story Jesus told Simon?

Think about a time you were given a gift of grace (either from God or another person, like my geometry story). How did it make you feel?

---

6   Luke 7 Matthew Henry's Commentary, https://bibleapps.com/mhc/luke/7.htm.

- Day 15 -
Forgiveness Leads To Compassion

Today's Bible Reading: Luke 7:36-50 (focus on verses 44-50)

Over the past five days, we've been looking at the story of The Unwelcome Dinner Guest. We've seen her courage as she risked public humiliation to get to the feet of Jesus. We've seen a Pharisee named Simon judge her harshly. And in response, we've heard Jesus tell a story of two debtors—a story that illustrates how experiencing forgiveness leads to an outpouring of love.

Now Jesus asks Simon a profound question: "Do you see this woman?"

Of course, Simon sees her. He sees her, and he's disgusted by her. But has he *really* seen her? Has he tried to look past his prejudices and judgments to see who this woman is? To really understand her story? There is a popular quote that says, "Be kind, for everyone you meet is fighting a great battle." (Although frequently attributed to Philo of Alexandria, no one is 100% sure who said it first. Those are the best kinds of quotes!) If Simon could only see a fraction of the battle this woman was fighting, maybe he would ease up a bit.

Then Jesus describes all the ways this woman has shown love to him. And he correlates that great love to the forgiveness she has experienced. He tells Simon:

Therefore, I tell you, her many sins have been forgiven—as her great love has shown. But whoever has been forgiven little loves little. (v. 47, NIV)

When Jesus says, "whoever has been forgiven little loves little," I don't think he's referring to the *number* of sins we've been forgiven for. I think he means the *way* we've experienced that forgiveness. If we realize we've been forgiven much, then forgiveness will lead to compassion.

In September 2018, Amber Guyger, a Dallas police officer, shot and killed Botham Jean in his own apartment. A year later, she was sentenced to 10 years in prison. After the sentencing, Brandt Jean—Botham's younger brother—extended forgiveness to Amber. This is what he said:

If you truly are sorry, I know… I can speak for myself, I forgive you. And I know if you go to God and ask him, he will forgive you. Again, I'm speaking for myself, not even on behalf of my family, but I love you, just like anyone else. I'm not going to say I hope you rot and die just like my brother did, but I, personally, want the best for you. I wasn't going to ever say this in front of my family or anyone, but I don't even want you to go to jail. I want the best for you, because I know that's exactly what Botham would want you to do. And the best would be, give your life to Christ.[7]

And then he embraced Amber in a hug. What led to such an unbelievable act of compassion?

Like the woman at Jesus' feet, I think Brandt Jean had been forgiven much. He knew he was a fellow debtor, released from his debt by God. Now he wants everyone else to experience that same freedom.

The story of The Unwelcome Dinner Guest is a reminder of how much we've been forgiven. When we remember how much debt we were in, how could we not have anything but compassion on the fellow debtors we meet?

---

7   Culver, Jordan. "'I Want the Best for You': Botham Jean's Brother Hugs Amber Guyger in Emotional Courtroom Scene." USA Today, October 3, 2019. https://www.usatoday.com/story/news/nation/2019/10/02/amber-guyger-sentencing-botham-jeans-brother-embraces-guyger/3847967002/.

💬 Questions to Ponder:

Do you see yourself as being forgiven little or being forgiven much? How does that influence the way you view others?

What is one thing you've learned about Jesus from the story of The Unwelcome Dinner Guest?

Encounter IV:
Jesus Meets The Woman
Who Was Exploited

Shouts echo throughout the temple courts. Religious men drag in a frightened woman, her head hanging in shame. They make a show of her in front of the crowd, exploiting her most vulnerable moment.

Then they make her face Jesus in an impromptu trial. They are using her sad situation to trap Jesus. Should she receive justice or mercy? You can't have it both ways.

Jesus ponders the riddle silently. Then, he gives an answer that shocks everyone.

* * *

You can find the story of The Woman Who Was Exploited in **John 8:2-11**. Take a few minutes to read it, and then we'll jump in!

- Day 16 -
The Woman Who Was Exploited

Today's Bible Reading: John 8:2-11
Supporting Passage: Matthew 9:9-13

For our next encounter, we'll be looking at the interaction between Jesus and a woman on trial for adultery. The Pharisees used this situation to put Jesus between a rock and a hard place. (Literally. They wanted his permission to stone her.) But, as he did with Simon, Jesus uses the scene to illustrate an important lesson on sin and grace.

Today, I want to highlight three caveats about this story before we dive into it:

1. This story is one of the most well-known stories about Jesus.

Because of that reason, I almost didn't include it in this book. How much can I say about a story that seems so straightforward? But I'm discovering that with Bible stories, there is always something more to learn. I'm amazed when I read a book or article that helps me see a biblical story in a new way. The Bible is like an old friend. You never run out of things to discuss! Familiar stories are worth revisiting for that reason.

This story also contains one of the most oft-quoted phrases of Jesus: "Let any one of you who is without sin be the first to throw a stone" (v. 7). Usually, we utter it when we want to justify *our own* behavior. Jesus may have had a deeper meaning in mind. We'll get to that in a few days.

2. There is a dispute about whether this story belongs in the Bible.

Your Bible may include a preface to this story that says something like:

The earliest manuscripts and many other ancient witnesses do not have John 7:53–8:11.

I'm no biblical scholar, so I'll leave that debate up to people who are smarter than me. All I'll say is this: Jesus' behavior in this story is very consistent with how he acts in similar scenarios. In the book of Matthew, the Pharisees grumble when they see Jesus eating with "sinners." Jesus replies, "It is not the healthy who need a doctor, but the sick." (Matthew 9:12, NIV) That's pretty much the theme of this story.

3. This story is often referenced as "The Woman Caught in Adultery." I prefer to call it "The Woman Who Was Exploited."

Why? Because once again, the Pharisees try to use someone to move their agenda forward. Yes, this woman committed adultery. She never denies that. But the Pharisees exploit her situation to set a trap for Jesus.

Oh, I should also mention a fourth thing I discovered recently: This story has a pretty shocking twist ending. (If you thought *The Sixth Sense* was good, wait until you see this one!) We'll unpack it in a few days.

🗨 Questions to Ponder:

Take some time to read John 8:2–11.

If you are familiar with this story, are there any new things that stand out to you?

If you are not familiar with this story, what is your main takeaway after reading it?

- Day 17 -
Joy Crushers

Today's Bible Reading: John 8:2-11
Supporting Passage: John 5:1-14

Have you ever been at a party when suddenly all the fun was sucked right out of the room by someone?

The music comes to a screeching halt. The room fills with awkward silence. You stop eating the pizza slice mid-bite. All heads turn to see who interrupted the festivities.

The Pharisees caused a scene like this when they brought the woman they chose to exploit to Jesus.

The people of Jerusalem were celebrating the Festival of Tabernacles, which took place in mid-October. Jesus was teaching at the festival, and opinions about him divided the audience. Some people thought he was a good man. Others thought he was a deceiver.

Even so, it was a joyful festival where everyone was having fun. Everyone, that is, except for the Pharisees. They were in their secret hideout, plotting how to get rid of Jesus.

A few chapters before this in John 5, Jesus healed a paralyzed man. Unfortunately, he made the "mistake" of healing on the Sabbath. That really got under the Pharisees' skin. Jesus seemed perplexed by their anger, asking them:

"Now if a boy can be circumcised on the Sabbath so that the law of Moses may

not be broken, why are you angry with me for healing a man's whole body on the Sabbath?" (John 7:23, NIV)

In other words, *why are you dudes being such Joy Crushers?*

This is the backdrop of our story. The stage is set for another show-down between Jesus and the Pharisees. And when the curtain comes up, they are dragging a frightened woman into the temple courts, making a scene at the festival for all to see.

Then, they set a perfect trap for Jesus while faking reverence:

"Teacher, this woman was caught in the act of adultery. In the Law Moses commanded us to stone such women. Now what do you say?" (John 8:4–5, NIV)

In the musical *Camelot,* King Arthur was put in a similar situation. He has worked all his life to create a land of law and order—peace and righteousness reign in Camelot. But when Queen Guenevere is caught in the act of adultery, the penalty is death.

Mordred, Arthur's wayward son, mocks him relentlessly.

"What a magnificent dilemma!" Mordred gloats. "Let her die, your life is over; let her live, your life's a fraud. Which will it be, Arthur? **Do you kill the Queen or kill the law?"**

The Pharisees thought they had put Jesus in a magnificent dilemma as well. If he lets the woman go, it's another piece of evidence that he doesn't care about the Law of Moses. If he says to stone her, he's turning his back on the "sinners" he claims to love so much.

But nobody puts Jesus in a corner.

💬 Questions to Ponder:

Does knowing more about the context of this story change the way you view it? (For more background about the festival, read John 7.)

What do you think of King Arthur's "Do you kill the Queen or kill the law?" dilemma? How would you solve it?

- Day 18 -
Ethical Twister

Today's Bible Reading: John 8:2-11 (focus on verses 2-6)
Supporting Passage: Genesis 38:12-26

One of my goals when writing this book was to approach Bible stories from all the characters' points of view. This means pointing out the flaws in the "heroes" and having empathy for the "villains." Today, I want to take a closer look at the Pharisees—the "Joy Crushers" who put this woman's shame on display for all to see.

The Pharisees were suggesting that the woman be stoned to death. That sounds like a horrible way to die, doesn't it? I've read this story so many times but never really let that image sink in. Think about it for a moment: throwing rocks at someone until they die. It's unfathomable.

To be fair, there is a good chance they were bluffing. Yes, the Law of Moses required adulterers to be stoned. But there is little evidence that this punishment was routinely carried out. Because they were under Roman rule, the Jewish leaders weren't allowed to perform executions. (That's why they needed Rome's help to kill Jesus.) Verse 6 says:

They were using this question as a trap, in order to have a basis for accusing him.
(NIV)

Chances are, the Pharisees were using this woman to pose a hypothetical question to Jesus. Still, that didn't make her fear and humiliation any less real.

Then there is the issue of the double standard. The last time I checked, adultery requires two willing participants. The New King James Version says the woman "was caught in adultery, *in the very act.*" (Emphasis mine.) That seems like a setup to me. Did they pay the man to take part in this scheme, promising he would remain anonymous? And if it *wasn't* a setup, well… then that seems even worse! How did they catch her "in the very act" unless they were looking somewhere they shouldn't be looking?

It reminds me of an odd story found in Genesis 38. A woman named Tamar disguises herself as a prostitute. She sleeps with Judah, her father-in-law, and becomes pregnant. Three months later, Judah gets word that Tamar is guilty of prostitution. Not realizing he's the reason she's pregnant, he orders her to be burned alive. How's that for hypocrisy? (Don't worry; when he found out the truth, he backed down.)

When you look at how many angles these Pharisees worked to get their way, it's hard to have empathy for them. And yet, how often do I play Ethical Twister to get my way? Maybe the Pharisees knew they were making compromises but thought the "greater good" justified it.

The amazing thing is, Jesus kept his cool. Tomorrow, we'll look at the gentle way he dealt with the Pharisees' hypocrisy. Jesus loved these men, just like he loved the woman. His response is more evidence that he doesn't want anyone left out.

💬 Questions to Ponder:

What similarities do you find between this story and the story in Genesis 38?

When are you most tempted to make compromises for the "greater good"?

Today, whether you feel more like the woman or more like the Pharisees, remember that Jesus loves you.

- Day 19 -
Don't Walk Away, Join The Party

Today's Bible Reading: John 8:2-11 (focus on verses 5-9)
Supporting Passage: Luke 15:25-32

This week, we've been looking at the interaction between Jesus and the woman accused of adultery. But so far, they haven't interacted yet. In fact, Jesus hasn't spoken a word to anyone. After the Pharisees bring the woman to Jesus, they await his response.

"In the Law, Moses commanded us to stone such women. What do you say?" they ask.

And now Jesus does something strange:

Jesus bent down and started to write on the ground with his finger. (v. 6, NIV)

A lot of smart people have tried to guess what Jesus was writing in the dirt. Some people say he was writing a verse from the Old Testament. Other people think he was writing down the sins of the Pharisees, pointing out that they had faults, too. I don't think we'll ever know until we meet Jesus in person. *(It will probably be the first question he addresses!)*

But you know what I think? I think he was doodling. He had just dealt with similar nonsense from the Pharisees a day earlier. Maybe he needed a moment to collect his thoughts, the way a parent needs to take a breath before dealing with a child.

And let's face it, the Pharisees *were* acting like children. They continue to impatiently badger Jesus with the question. Finally, Jesus looks at them and says the famous line:

"Let any one of you who is without sin be the first to throw a stone at her." (v. 7, NIV)

Jesus was inviting them to examine themselves before condemning others. And after a few awkward moments, the Pharisees begin to walk away, one at a time.

As I've thought about this, one question keeps popping up in my mind. Why did these men walk away? If they were so self-righteous, then why didn't they pick up a stone and start executing judgment?

The Pharisees were smart. They studied God's law meticulously. And even though they held a high opinion of themselves, they knew they weren't without sin.

Jesus' response is often quoted in pop culture. But we need to remember it isn't a convenient excuse to use when we want to justify our behavior. It's the opposite—a call to look inward.

I think the saddest part of this story is that the Pharisees walked away. When confronted with their brokenness, they chose to leave, seething in anger. Their opinion of Jesus only grew worse because of this incident.

The Pharisees remind me of the older brother in the Prodigal Son story. After he sees his father welcome home his younger brother, he's furious. And even though he's invited to the celebration party, he refuses to attend.

Can you imagine if, after realizing their own sin, these men fell to the ground in sorrow? Can you imagine if they asked the woman for forgiveness for exploiting her in this way? What a beautiful picture that would have been.

Jesus was about to throw this woman a welcome home party. And, although they were invited, the Pharisees chose to walk away.

 Questions to Ponder:

Why do you think the Pharisees walked away?

How can examining our own brokenness move us toward others rather than away from them?

- Day 20 -
The Surprise Ending

Today's Bible Reading: John 8:2-11 (focus on verses 10-11)
Supporting Passage: Isaiah 53:5

Over the past five days, we've spent time looking at the story of the woman who was exploited by Pharisees. We've witnessed the Pharisees drag her to Jesus in an attempt to trip him up. And we've seen Jesus remind the men of their own sin, causing them to walk away callously.

Now, Jesus and the woman stand face to face. No doubt, the woman is still afraid. But here's how the story ends:

Jesus straightened up and asked her, "Woman, where are they? Has no one condemned you?"

"No one, sir," she said.

"Then neither do I condemn you," Jesus declared. "Go now and leave your life of sin." (v. 10–11, NIV)

Sometimes hearing Jesus say, "I do not condemn you" is difficult for me to accept. It's much easier for me to wallow in shame than believe Jesus has forgiven me. But Jesus doesn't scold this woman. He doesn't make her relive all the events leading up to this moment. He simply gives her grace.

But what about Jesus' last words to her? "Go now and leave your life of sin." That seems like a tall order. Even as he said those words, Jesus knew he was asking for the impossible. 1 John 1:8 says, "If we claim to be without sin, we deceive ourselves and the truth is not in us" (NIV).

So if we can't stop sinning, but the bar set by Jesus is to never sin again, what do we do?

Earlier this week, I mentioned the "King Arthur" dilemma: Queen Guenevere has committed adultery, and now Arthur must decide whether to "kill the Queen or kill the law." His solution? He goes through the motions of an execution. At the last moment, before Guenevere is burned alive, he allows Lancelot's army to storm Camelot and rescue her. Guenevere is saved, but a whole kingdom is destroyed in the process. Other people pay dearly for her freedom.

Jesus has a better solution. It leads to peace, not destruction. But it will cost him everything. The surprise twist in this story is that there *was* a stoning. It didn't happen that day, but it would happen soon. Jesus would be pelted by the heavy stones of our sin.

But he was pierced for our transgressions,
he was crushed for our iniquities;
the punishment that brought us peace was on him,
and by his wounds we are healed. (Isaiah 53:5, NIV)

Jesus told the woman she wasn't condemned. But that didn't mean her actions had no consequences. Jesus was saying, "You go, and I'll stay and take the stoning for you."

He extends this offer to all of us. Jesus will take the stoning for anyone willing to recognize their brokenness. He will shield us from the stones because he doesn't want anyone left out.

💬 Questions to Ponder:

Is it difficult for you to accept that Jesus doesn't condemn you for past mistakes? If so, thank Jesus for his grace and ask him to help you move forward in freedom.

What do you think of the concept of Jesus "taking the stoning for you"?

What is one thing you've learned about Jesus from the story of The Woman Who Was Exploited?

Encounter V:
Jesus Meets The Sick Woman
& The Dead Girl

*We lead such busy lives. On most days, our schedules
are packed to the brim, leaving little room for surprise
interruptions. Jesus also had a tight schedule, but you
wouldn't have known it from the way he moseyed
about. Some people were frustrated by his slow pace.*

*One day an important man begged Jesus for help—
his little daughter was dying. Jesus goes, but along
the way he gets interrupted by a woman who
everyone else had forgotten. His disciples tried to
hurry him along, but Jesus refused to be rushed.*

On that day, Jesus turned panic and chaos into hope and joy.

* * *

You can find the story of The Sick Woman & The Dead Girl
in **Mark 5:21-43**. Take a few minutes to read it, and then
we'll jump in!

- Day 21 -
The Faith Of A Sick Woman
& Joy Of A Dead Girl

Today's Bible Reading: Mark 5:21-43

For our next encounter, we're getting two stories for the price of one! In Mark 5:21–43, two interactions with Jesus are woven together to create one beautiful tapestry.

Mark is the shortest gospel, and it's all about showing Jesus in action. I'm not surprised that Mark saved ink on the page by telling these two stories side by side. And yet, the stories are connected. They almost mirror each other.

Before going any further, please take some time to read the full passage. It's a bit lengthier than usual, but having the full scope of the story will help us as we begin to look at each section.

At the center of the story are two women. One has been battling a medical illness every day for twelve years. The other is on her death-bed at only twelve years old. Is twelve years a long time? I guess that depends on who you ask. For the woman, the past twelve years have been excruciatingly long. For the girl (and her parents), twelve years went by like a vapor of mist.

But despite their terrible situations, these two women lift my spirits. Their stories play out like a comedy, and I can't help but smile when I get to the end. Chaos surrounds the women on all sides—pushy crowds, sarcastic disciples, and busybody neighbors. And yet, surrounded by all that negativity, faith and joy still manage to win the day.

The sick woman had the faith to go to Jesus, even when every other avenue of healing she tried was a dead end. Her faith is staggering: *"If I just touch his clothes, I will be healed"* (v. 28, NIV). After so many disappointments, she still has confidence in Jesus.

Then you have the joy of the dead girl. After Jesus raises her to life, she's up and walking around, going about her day as usual. And how do you celebrate any happy occasion? With a meal, of course. Jesus tells her parents to get this girl something to eat!

These two stories remind me that Jesus is in control even when everyone else is in panic mode. They are stories of hope. And we all face circumstances that could use a little dose of hope to get us through.

💬 Questions to Ponder:

As you read this passage, list all the instances where faith and joy win out over chaos and panic.

What is one circumstance you are facing where you need to be reminded that Jesus is in control?

- Day 22 -
Competing For Jesus' Attention

Today's Bible Reading: Mark 5:21-43 (focus on verses 21-24)
Supporting Passage: John 16:5-7

Large crowds can be a scary thing. I am not a fan of them, especially when the bumping and shoving start happening. I don't have the best balance because of my cerebral palsy and can easily fall over. (In middle school, I was allowed to leave each class five minutes early to avoid the swarm of kids in the hallways!)

In the Gospel of Mark, Jesus attracts large crowds wherever he goes. Every now and then, he does something to freak out the crowd, causing them to turn on him. Right before Jesus heals the sick woman in our story, he heals a demon-possessed man in the next town over (Mark 5:1–20). The townspeople are so afraid to see this crazed man in his right mind that they beg Jesus to leave (a reminder that sometimes we reject Jesus even when he does amazing things!). But as soon as Jesus crosses to the other side of the lake, another crowd starts forming around him.

This is where we are introduced to the first character in our story: the father of the dying girl. His name is Jairus, and he is a leader at a local synagogue. That means he's one of the few religious leaders who are not opposed to Jesus. While not a Pharisee, Jairus was responsible for the day-to-day operations of running the synagogue. And when tragedy strikes at home, he risks his public image to seek out Jesus and plead for the life of his little girl. Jairus was a good man.

But how did Jairus get to Jesus? A crowd had already gathered around Jesus before Jairus came. Did he fight his way to the front? Or did the crowd part like the Red Sea for this important member of the community to come through? I'm sure everyone knew who Jairus was. If Jairus wanted to get to Jesus, then Jairus was going to get to Jesus.

This story reminds me that when Jesus walked this earth, he couldn't get to everyone who needed him. He was fully God but constrained by time and space. (I'd imagine that was frustrating for him.) There were people in that crowd who desperately wanted to get to Jesus. I'm sure there were people who were disappointed when Jesus said "yes" to going with Jairus. "Of course, Jairus, the important synagogue leader, gets Jesus' attention..."

I think this is why Jesus was so excited for his followers to meet the Holy Spirit. Right before he was crucified, he told them:

Unless I go away, the Advocate will not come to you; but if I go, I will send him to you. (John 16:7, NIV)

What could be better than having Jesus with us on this earth? Having access to Jesus 24/7 through his Spirit. We don't have to compete for Jesus' attention.

But sometimes it feels like we do, doesn't it? Sometimes, it feels like there are "Jairuses" all around us—people who are more worthy of Jesus' attention than we are. People who Jesus is more inclined to go with.

But that's not true. There's no need to push your way to the front of the crowd. Jesus is with you right now. As the most famous verse says (John 3:16), Jesus has enough love for the whole world.

💬 Questions to Ponder:

What do you think it would have been like to be in the crowd around Jesus?

Do you ever feel like you have to compete for Jesus' attention?

- Day 23 -
One Miracle Away From Being An Atheist

Today's Bible Reading: Mark 5:21-43 (focus on verses 24-34)

A guest pastor came to speak a few months ago at a church staff meeting. As he shared his story, he made a statement that I found intriguing: "There was a time in my life when I was one miracle away from becoming an atheist."

He went on to explain that his son was sick from birth, and although he prayed fervently, his son wasn't improving. And yet, God seemed to be moving and working in the lives of others. "It got to a point where if God did one more miracle for someone else, I would have to stop believing in him," he explained.

I wonder if the woman in our story ever felt like that during the twelve years she was sick.

The crowd follows Jesus as he heads to Jairus's house. Hidden in the group, this woman starts to make her way toward Jesus. She's heard the rumors that this man heals people. And she believes them. She may never be this close to Jesus again, so it's now or never. She stretches out her hand, desperate to reach him.

In many ways, this woman represented the opposite of Jairus. He was a well-respected man, a local community leader. She had an illness that ostracized her from the community. Because it prevented her from bearing children, she was probably not married. She spent all she had to get better, draining her finances, health, and emotions. What kept her going all those years? Why didn't she give up?

The moment she touches his cloak, Jesus stops in his tracks. "Who touched my clothes?" he asks. And then the disciples get snarky with Jesus:

"You see the people crowding against you," his disciples answered, "and yet you can ask, 'Who touched me?'" (v. 31, NIV)

In other words: "Jesus, we're tired, we're hungry, we're sick of all these crowds, and we still have to get to Jairus's house… You see how many people are bumping into you… How can you ask, 'Who touched me?' Who even cares?!"

Jesus cares. Jesus always stops to see people who are overlooked. He hits the pause button on helping an important leader to help a woman who nobody else values. And when the truth comes out and the woman steps forward, Jesus commends her in front of everyone:

He said to her, "Daughter, your faith has healed you. Go in peace and be freed from your suffering." (v. 34, NIV)

I think it's beautiful that Jesus calls her "Daughter." It echoes the words of Jairus only a few verses earlier:

My little daughter is dying. Please come and put your hands on her so that she will be healed and live. (v. 23, NIV, emphasis mine)

The woman didn't have anyone to go to bat for her the way Jairus's daughter did. But now Jesus includes her in his family.

Questions to Ponder:

Have you ever been one miracle away from becoming an atheist? How can you stay focused on Jesus even when you can't see God at work?

Is there anyone you have been overlooking? How can you hit the "pause button" on life and see them the way Jesus would?

- Day 24 -
Ruthless Trust

Today's Bible Reading: Mark 5:21-43 (focus on verses 35-36)

Yesterday, we saw how Jesus' mission to save a dying girl was interrupted by a sick woman. She experienced disappointment for twelve years until grasping at Jesus' cloak finally healed her. I wonder how Jairus, the girl's father, felt about this interruption. Was he happy for the woman? Or was he trying to coax Jesus along? *Come on, Jesus, we haven't got much time… every minute you spend with this woman is one minute closer to my daughter's death!*

Soon, Jairus's worst fears are confirmed:

While Jesus was still speaking, some people came from the house of Jairus, the synagogue leader. "Your daughter is dead," they said. "Why bother the teacher anymore?" (v. 35, NIV)

Now it's Jairus's turn to experience disappointment. Jesus was too late. Time had run out. Does Jesus have a daily limit for miracles? A daily limit for compassion? Sometimes I wonder if I reach my daily limit for compassion too early in the day.

Unfazed by all this, Jesus whispers to Jairus. "Don't be afraid; just believe."

Jesus was asking Jairus to trust him. It wasn't blind trust—Jairus had just seen Jesus heal the sick woman. But it was still a lot to ask. Jairus's daughter is dead. There's not even the slightest shred of hope to cling to. And yet, Jairus dares to trust. He continues on with Jesus.

I hate roller coasters, but I've ridden a few in my life. During the scariest moments, all I can do is close my eyes, put my head down, and grit my teeth. Just when I think I can't tolerate it anymore—just when I think I'm going to die—the coaster slows down, giving me a moment to recoup. After a breather, it's time for another loop! That's what trusting Jesus feels like. Brennan Manning calls it a *Ruthless Trust*. In his book of the same name, he says:

In the midst of the ruins—in the premature death of a loved one, in the hell on earth we call a crack house, in the ache of a heartbreak, in the sheer malevolence of Kosovo and Rwanda—the presence of God abides. The trusting disciple, often through clenched teeth, says, in effect, God is still trustworthy, but not because of unrestricted power on my behalf, he is trustworthy because of a promise given and sustained in Christian communities throughout generations.[8]

And what is that promise? Manning says it's the promise that "during our desolate hours there would be one set of footprints."

It's the promise that Jesus is with us, carrying us through our darkest times. It's the promise that Jesus is in the roller coaster seat next to me. No, scratch that. It's the promise that Jesus is holding me in his lap on the roller coaster!

Ruthless Trust says that even when all hope seems lost, I can still cling to Jesus.

---

8   Manning, Brennan. *Ruthless Trust: the Ragamuffin's Path to God.* New York, NY: HarperCollins e-books, 2010.

💬 Questions to Ponder:

How soon do you reach your "daily limit for compassion"? Is there any way to refuel your compassion tank?

If you were Jairus, would it be hard or easy to trust Jesus? What is one thing you need to trust Jesus with this week?

- Day 25 -
Glimpse Into Eternity

Today's Bible Reading: Mark 5:21-43 (focus on verses 37-43)

Over the past five days, we've been looking at two interwoven stories. We've seen Jairus, a local leader, beg Jesus to heal his dying daughter. When they are interrupted along the way by a sick woman, Jesus hits the pause button to help. Now, thanks to the delay, Jairus's daughter is dead. Undeterred, Jesus asks Jairus to trust him.

When they arrive at Jairus's house, they find quite a scene:

When they came to the home of the synagogue leader, Jesus saw a commotion, with people crying and wailing loudly. He went in and said to them, "Why all this commotion and wailing? The child is not dead but asleep." But they laughed at him. (v. 38–40, NIV)

It's kind of ironic. Jesus turned the crowd's mourning into laughter before even performing a miracle. Of course, it was sarcastic laughter. We can't really blame them for thinking Jesus was out of his mind. The girl was dead, and that's a fact. But, as J. Ellsworth Kalas says in his book *Grace in a Tree Stump*, "Grace is wonderfully unknowing of life's facts."[9]

Then, Jesus takes the girl's father and mother into the house and does the impossible. He commands Death to release its grip from the girl:

---

9 Kalas, J. Ellsworth. *Grace in a Tree Stump: Old Testament Stories of God's Love*. Louisville, KY: Westminster John Knox Press, 2005.

He took her by the hand and said to her, "Talitha koum!" (which means "Little girl, I say to you, get up!"). Immediately the girl stood up and began to walk around (she was twelve years old). At this they were completely astonished. (v. 41–42, NIV)

And then Jesus throws a celebration party in honor of the girl, complete with food. I imagine him exiting the house and looking over at the crowd who had just laughed at him. He gives a little smile, gestures to the doorway, and says, "The Jairus family is having a little shindig. You're all invited." It was the first-ever celebration of life ceremony. And when the crowd sees the little girl up and running around, they laugh. It's no longer sarcastic laughter. It's joyful laughter.

It's easy to read a story like this and think, *Okay, good for them, but what about us?* We've all lost someone dear to us, and Jesus didn't raise them back to life. But this story is a glimpse into eternity. Jesus was giving us a window into what it will look like when he sets all things right. He was showing his power over Death. A day is coming when Jesus will put Death in its grave for good, and mourning will turn into joyful laughter.

I imagine it will be quite a celebration!

💬 Questions to Ponder:

Does Jesus' "glimpse into eternity" give you hope for the future? Why or why not?

What are you most looking forward to when Jesus ultimately sets all things right?

What is one thing you've learned about Jesus from the story of The Sick Woman & The Dead Girl?

Encounter VI:
Jesus Meets The Blind Man
With Perfect Vision

We live in a world where suffering is a reality. Well-meaning platitudes fall short when there is so much pain around us. We want to know why bad things happen.

When Jesus' disciples came across a man born blind, they wanted to know why, too. They saw him as a theological puzzle to be solved—who deserves the blame for his suffering? But they were asking the wrong question. Through this encounter, Jesus reveals that God is found in the broken places, the messy places, the painful places.

Jesus healed the blind man and, in the process, opened up everyone else's eyes.

* * *

You can find the story of The Blind Man With Perfect Vision in **John 9**. Take a few minutes to read it, and then we'll jump in!

- Day 26 -
Readjusting Our Vision

Today's Bible Reading: John 9

For our next encounter, we'll be looking at Jesus' interaction with a man born blind and the fallout that happens when Jesus heals him. This is one of my favorite stories in the Bible, and it takes up the entire chapter of John 9. I love this story because it challenges our vision of God. By bringing sight to a blind man, Jesus also readjusts everyone else's vision.

Today, I want to highlight three common perceptions Jesus obliterates through this interaction:

1. Suffering Is Due to Sin

As someone born with a disability, this story has always brought me comfort. The disciples saw this man's blindness as a theological puzzle to be solved. "Who sinned?" they ask Jesus. "This man or his parents?" In their worldview, sin and suffering are connected. If you were born with a disability or lived in poverty or contracted a disease, then you must have done something wrong. You made God mad and were being punished. Jesus challenges this view and gives us a new way to look at suffering.

I love that Jesus confronted this topic head-on. Jesus' public ministry was short, and he didn't address every single question we have about God. But he knew that the problem of suffering would be an important one. More on this topic tomorrow.

2. Things Can Only Be Set Right in Heaven

The second perception this story challenges is our response to suffering. In modern Christianity, there are a lot of phrases like *this world is not my home* or *I'm just passing through*. These phrases are meant to bring comfort in suffering, and it's true that someday God will set all things right. But it's also true that we can roll up our sleeves and do good *now*.

Jesus didn't look at this man and say, "Yes, this poor man is suffering now, but don't worry. Someday, God will fix this." No. Jesus got his hands dirty and helped him. As 19th-century preacher Charles Spurgeon said:

It is ours, not to speculate, but to perform acts of mercy and love, according to the tenor of the gospel. Let us then be less inquisitive and more practical, less for cracking doctrinal nuts, and more for bringing forth the bread of life to the starving multitudes.

We may not be able to heal people the way Jesus did. But we can love and serve them. We can be part of God's kingdom on earth. Sometimes the most "spiritual" thing to do in a situation is the most practical thing.

3. Certainty Is the Path to God

The last perception that Jesus overturns is how we get to God. The Pharisees chose a path of pride. They were so confident they knew how God worked that they missed what God was doing entirely. They were blinded by arrogance.

The man born blind discovered that the road to God is broken and messy. But it's also one where Jesus walks alongside us.

💬 Questions to Ponder:

Today, take some time to read John 9. What are some things that stand out to you?

Does this story change any of your perceptions about how God or the world operates?

- Day 27 -
The Oldest Question

Today's Bible Reading: John 9 (focus on verses 1-5)
Supporting Passage: Habakkuk 1:1-4

If God is so good, then why is there so much suffering in this world?

At some point in our lives, I'm sure we've all asked that question. Some people use the question as an excuse to not believe in God. They pose it as a "Gotcha!" and are not really interested in finding an answer. Other people ask the question with all sincerity. They want to believe in God, but they have experienced so much heartbreak in life. They can't understand why a loving God would allow his children to suffer.

This question, while important, is not a new one. In the Old Testament, the prophet Habakkuk (which, by the way, is an awesome name!) gets into an argument with God about all the suffering he sees in the world. He cries out:

"How long, Lord, must I call for help,
but you do not listen?
Or cry out to you, 'Violence!'
but you do not save?" (Habakkuk 1:1–2, NIV)

When Jesus comes across the man born blind, his disciples come up with their own theory to answer the question: Somebody did something wrong.

As he went along, [Jesus] saw a man blind from birth. His disciples asked him, *"Rabbi, who sinned, this man or his parents, that he was born blind?"* (John 9:1–2, NIV)

I always thought it was weird that the disciples blamed the man. After all, if the man was *born* blind, then when would he have sinned to deserve this punishment? As I've researched this story, I came across a few possibilities.

At that time, some people believed in a form of reincarnation. Maybe the man sinned in a previous life. Others thought a baby could sin while still in the womb. A third option is the man was being punished for a future sin he would commit. Whatever their reasoning, the disciples had it all figured out. It was either the blind man's fault or his parents' fault.

Whenever people asked Jesus an "either/or" question, he usually widened their view of the situation. Instead of blaming someone, Jesus challenged his disciples to look for God amid the suffering. The Message version of the Bible puts Jesus' answer this way:

Jesus said, "You're asking the wrong question. You're looking for someone to blame. There is no such cause-effect here. Look instead for what God can do." (John 9:3)

Years ago, I was at Walmart rummaging through some CDs. A woman approached me and asked if she could pray for me. I said yes. I will always accept prayer! As the woman prayed, she asked God to heal me of my disability. Her prayer grew louder and louder, and when she finished, she said, "Now you have to believe!"

In her view, the greatest good was that I would be healed of my cerebral palsy. And if God chose to do that, I would happily accept! But I've seen God do amazing things in my life. And I've watched other people go through terrible times and come out with a renewed sense of purpose. God can be found in life's darkest moments.

Even if we fully understood the "why" of suffering, we still wouldn't

75

like it. But we have a God who chose to leave his perfect home, put on human flesh, and experience human suffering with us.

 Questions to Ponder:

If God is so good, then why is there so much suffering in this world? What do you think? Have you ever asked some form of this—the world's "Oldest Question"?

What do you think of the concept of God (as Jesus) experiencing suffering alongside us?

Where have you seen God show up in your suffering?

- Day 28 -
I Was Blind, But Now I See

Today's Bible Reading: John 9 (focus on verses 6-25)

Amazing Grace, how sweet the sound
That saved a wretch like me
I once was lost, but now am found
'Twas blind but now I see[10]

Most people are familiar with the opening verse of "Amazing Grace." In 11th grade, I sang it at an audition for *Bye, Bye, Birdie**. But it wasn't until much later that I realized that the famous "'Twas blind but now I see" line came from this Bible story.

After Jesus gives the disciples a new perspective on suffering, he gets to work. He makes some mud, puts it on the blind man's eyes, and gives him the gift of sight. For the first time in his life, the man can see. And this is where things get interesting.

Whenever Jesus healed someone, people became skeptical. Instead of being happy for the man, his neighbors dragged him to the Pharisees. Jesus healed him on the Sabbath, which was a big no-no. (I think Jesus loved healing people on the Sabbath just to get under the Pharisees' skin. If you wanted Jesus to heal you, the best time to see him was on the Sabbath!)

The Pharisees ask the man how he got his sight back, and the man simply gives them the facts: "He put mud on my eyes, and I washed,

---

10   Newton, John. *Amazing Grace*

and now I see." This answer is not good enough for the Pharisees, and they continue to ask the same question over and over. At one point, they even bring in the man's parents to answer for him! (I can relate to this part. I remember being at restaurants with my parents, and the waiter, seeing I had a disability, would ask them, "And what will *he* have?" My dad would shrug and say, "I don't know, ask him.")

The Pharisees already had their minds made up about Jesus. They were asking questions but not really looking for answers. How often do we do this? It used to be that we watched political debates to gain insight into candidates. Now, we watch them more like sporting events. Will our favorite "team" win?

By contrast, the man born blind is quite comfortable not having all the answers. When the Pharisees try to get him to call Jesus a sinner, he says his famous line:

"Whether he is a sinner or not, I don't know. One thing I do know. I was blind but now I see!" (v. 25, NIV)

In other words, I don't know everything there is to know about Jesus, but I want to know more. Send me the no-obligation info kit!

He didn't have all the right theology about Jesus yet. But he had joy about what Jesus did for him. And that was enough to start taking small steps toward following him.

We don't need to understand everything about Jesus before we start following him, either. With any relationship, it takes time to get to know the other person. Jesus invites us all to get to know him because he doesn't want anyone left out.

> ### 💬 Questions to Ponder:
>
> Have you ever asked questions when you weren't really looking for answers? Rather than getting defensive when confronted with an opposing view, how can you become curious?
>
> In verse 25, the man born blind admits something he doesn't know about Jesus. What is something you don't fully know or understand about Jesus? Can you choose to follow him anyway?

* *For those who were curious, I was cast in* Bye, Bye, Birdie *as Mr. Johnson, Harvey Johnson's father!*

- Day 29 -
Too Smart To Be Joyful

Today's Bible Reading: John 9 (focus on verses 26-34)
Supporting Passage: 1 Corinthians 13:1-3

Yesterday, we saw how the (formerly) blind man responded when the Pharisees questioned him about Jesus. He didn't know everything about Jesus, but he knew one thing: Jesus healed him.

This response isn't good enough for the Pharisees. They continue to ask how Jesus healed him. Finally, the man gets so fed up with their questions that he hits back, with a bit of sarcasm thrown in for good measure:

He answered, "I have told you already and you did not listen. Why do you want to hear it again? Do you want to become his disciples too?" (v. 27, **NIV**)

This is where the Pharisees lose their cool. Their pride turns to anger, and their true feelings about this man are revealed:

To this they replied, "You were steeped in sin at birth; how dare you lecture us!" And they threw him out. (v. 34, **NIV**)

There is so much hatred wrapped up in those words. Their egos were bruised, and that's the perfect catalyst for turning pride into anger. (I know from experience!)

The Pharisees were essentially saying, *What do you know about God? We've studied him all our lives. We are clean, you are dirty. We are right, you are wrong. Who are you to try to teach us?*

80

The Pharisees were so caught up in the knowledge of God that they missed the joy of God. They couldn't (or wouldn't) acknowledge the beautiful thing Jesus did for this man.

Remember when you were a kid and got into a fight with one of your friends? You would cover your ears and shout, "I can't hear you! I can't hear you!" That's what the Pharisees did. They threw this man out of the temple because of a disagreement.

Some time ago, a well-known pastor was asked his opinion of a female Bible teacher. He summed up his answer in two words: "Go home." He was so confident in his view that there was no room for discussion. End of story. Case closed.

When we insist we have all the answers, we miss out on what God is doing. And that's a scary place to be. Even when our theology is correct, it doesn't matter one bit if we use it to steamroll others. As the Apostle Paul says:

If I speak in the tongues of men or of angels, but do not have love, I am only a resounding gong or a clanging cymbal. If I have the gift of prophecy and can fathom all mysteries and all knowledge, and if I have a faith that can move mountains, but do not have love, I am nothing. (1 Corinthians 13:1–2, NIV)

The Pharisees claimed to know everything about God, yet they were full of pride and anger. More than anything, it's sad that they missed an opportunity to celebrate with this man.

This story challenges me to examine my own life. Where do I allow pride to keep me from seeing God? When I have disagreements with others, am I allowing love to guide the conversation? Or do I just sound like a clanging cymbal?

Questions to Ponder:

Why do you think the Pharisees threw the man out of the temple?

Have you ever let a bruised ego turn your pride into anger? How can you allow love to guide you in disagreements?

- Day 30 -
The God Of Paradoxes

Today's Bible Reading: John 9 (focus on verses 35-41)
Supporting Passage: John 10:11-15

Over the past five days, we've been looking at the interaction between Jesus and the man born blind. We've seen Jesus heal the man and, in the process, readjust everyone else's vision. And we've seen the Pharisees get so angry that they throw the man out of the temple.

Now, in a beautiful twist of irony, Jesus pursues the man. The man is thrown out of God's house, only to be found by God in the flesh. Stories like this are why I love Jesus.

Jesus and the man share a tender moment. Jesus asks if he believes in the "Son of Man" (this was a phrase used to describe the promised Messiah). The man continues to be honest—he doesn't know who the Son of Man is. And then Jesus opens his eyes a second time:

Jesus said, "You have now seen him; in fact, he is the one speaking with you." Then the man said, "Lord, I believe," and he worshiped him. Jesus said, "For judgment I have come into this world, so that the blind will see and those who see will become blind." (v. 37–39, NIV)

What happens next makes me laugh when I imagine it. Have you ever watched a scene in a movie where two people are sharing an intimate moment, and it appears they are alone? But then the camera zooms out to reveal a ton of people standing awkwardly around them. That's what happens here!

The camera zooms out on this tender moment to reveal—you guessed it!—more Pharisees. They continue to lean into their arrogance:

Some Pharisees who were with him heard him say this and asked, "What? Are we blind too?" (v. 40, NIV)

Throughout this whole story, the man born blind has been open about his uncertainties. And yet he is the one who accepts Jesus. Meanwhile, the righteous Pharisees have shut themselves off from God.

John 9 ends with Jesus confronting the Pharisees about their spiritual blindness. But the story doesn't end there. His speech continues into chapter 10, where he calls himself the good shepherd:

I am the good shepherd; I know my sheep and my sheep know me...and I lay down my life for the sheep. (v. 14–15, NIV)

A blind man who can see. Seeing people who are blind. Finding truth in uncertainty. A man found by God after getting kicked out of God's house. This story is full of paradoxes.

But then I guess the whole story of Jesus is one big paradox, isn't it? The God of the universe coming to earth as a baby. Born in a dirty stable to a couple on the lowest rung of society. Spending time with the weak, the lonely, the forgotten. A good shepherd who allows himself to be devoured by wolves so that his sheep can live.

I said it before, but it's worth saying again: Stories like this are why I love Jesus.

 Questions to Ponder:

What paradoxes or unexpected moments do you find in this story?

What is one thing you've learned about Jesus from the story of The Blind Man With Perfect Vision?

Encounter VII:
Jesus Sees The Invisible Widow

People are usually pretty good at making their own messes. But sometimes, people are thrown into a mess through no fault of their own. They get trapped in unjust systems and are set up to fail by people in power. The most vulnerable among us who should be protected are often the most forgotten.

But they are not forgotten by Jesus. When a widow dropped a couple of cents into an offering basket, the world rolled on without giving her a second thought. But Jesus took notice. And not only did Jesus notice her, but he marveled at her—he marveled at this invisible widow.

And as the widow walked away, Jesus made sure her story would always be told.

* * *

You can find the story of The Invisible Widow in **Mark 12:41-44**. Take a few minutes to read it, and then we'll jump in!

- Day 31 -
Caught In The Act

Today's Bible Reading: Mark 12:41-44

So far, we've looked at six different encounters Jesus had with people. In each story, Jesus came into contact with someone and changed them in some way. But this next encounter is a little different. In this one, the main character doesn't actually interact with Jesus at all.

In Mark 12, we meet a poor widow who makes a generous offering at church. Jesus takes notice of her, but she never sees Jesus. She's completely unaware that her act is about to be immortalized in the pages of the Bible.

Here is her story, told in four short verses:

Jesus sat down opposite the place where the offerings were put and watched the crowd putting their money into the temple treasury. Many rich people threw in large amounts. But a poor widow came and put in two very small copper coins, worth only a few cents.

Calling his disciples to him, Jesus said, "Truly I tell you, this poor widow has put more into the treasury than all the others. They all gave out of their wealth; but she, out of her poverty, put in everything—all she had to live on." (Mark 12:41–44, NIV)

I used to think this was a simple story about money. The lesson is to be generous and give away as much money as possible, right? While generosity is important, I think Jesus is calling our attention to something more profound. The story of The Invisible Widow reminds me that God sees every single act of faithfulness.

Interestingly, Jesus doesn't give us a command in this story. He doesn't look at his disciples and say, *See how this woman gave everything she had? Now, go and do likewise.* Jesus doesn't ask us to drop every last penny into the offering basket as the widow did. Neither does he reprimand the rich people for not giving more.

Jesus was simply taking time out of his day to notice a beautiful act done by a poor widow. And he didn't just see her—he marveled at her. He was so moved by her act that he called over his disciples to witness the event with him.

Meanwhile, the widow had no idea Jesus was watching. She wasn't seeking attention. Her motivation wasn't to blow up on social media (#WatchMeGiveItAll). I'm sure this wasn't the first day she gave so generously. Her life was made up of ordinary days, taking steps of quiet faithfulness.

On this day, she happened to be caught in the act.

💬 Questions to Ponder:

How do you think this woman would feel to know her story has inspired millions of people?

Have you ever "caught someone in the act" of being faithful? How did it inspire you?

- Day 32 -
Every Story Matters

Today's Bible Reading: Mark 12:41-44

My wife, Diana, and I love to visit St. Augustine, Florida. We usually hop on a trolley that travels to 26 different places in the historic district. You can get on and off the trolley all day long. One of my favorite stops is the Memorial Presbyterian Church. It has a gorgeous sanctuary funded by Henry Flagler (the guy who owned pretty much all of St. Augustine) in 1890.

I love visiting the church later in the day when I'm tired from walking all around town. It's nice to sit and rest in a quiet place. The church is always full, but sitting in the pews still brings a sense of peace to a busy day.

Maybe this is how Jesus felt when he sat in the temple that day. It had been a long day of teaching and answering trick questions from the Pharisees. Earlier in the day, he was almost arrested for speaking against the chief priests (Mark 12:12). Now, finally, Jesus gets a quiet moment to himself. He sits down and watches as people come and go, putting money into the offering boxes that lined the walls. Jesus' eyes begin to droop as the exhaustion of the day catches up to him. And then he sees the widow walk up to one of the boxes and drop in her small offering.

Jesus calls his disciples over to witness this. I wonder, where were they before this? Were they wandering around the temple watching the rich people give their offerings? I can imagine them whispering, "Man, did you hear the clankety-clank of *that* offering? He's making bank! I wonder what his story is!"

Then, Jesus draws their attention to this poor widow. He reminds them that she has a story, too. She has a story about how she became widowed. She has a story about why she's choosing to give out of her poverty. And her story matters.

We are drawn to exciting stories. We want to know how the rich got rich and the famous got famous. It's why biopics are so popular.

When you ride the trolley around St. Augustine, you learn all about the life of Henry Flagler. How he struck it rich in the oil business and then built hotels and railroads in Florida. He died in 1913 with a net worth of $60 million (which I'm pretty sure is the equivalent of a bajillion dollars today). His story is fascinating.

But the next time I visit Memorial Presbyterian Church, I want to think about the widow's story. As I'm admiring the majestic sanctuary built by Mr. Flagler, I want to imagine what Jesus saw that day. A poor widow approaching the offering box and quietly dropping in two copper coins. Her story is fascinating, too.

Every story matters to Jesus because every person matters to Jesus. He doesn't want any story left out.

🗨 Questions to Ponder:

Jesus' disciples overlooked the widow and her story. Is there anyone whose story you have overlooked or dismissed? How can you invite them to share their story with you?

Have you ever thought your life story wasn't "exciting" enough? Today, take some time to remember that Jesus cares about every part of your story.

- Day 33 -
Faithfulness Matters

Today's Bible Reading: Mark 12:41-44
Supporting Passage: Job 1:1-12

Over the past couple of days, we've been looking at the story of The Invisible Widow. We've seen how the widow gave all she had even though she didn't think anyone was watching. Her life was made up of quiet days of faithfulness.

"Faithfulness" sounds like a churchy word. I don't know what images pop into your brain when you hear it. Maybe it has a negative connotation. Maybe someone has said, "You just need to trust God and keep being faithful." And you have. But it's getting hard, and you're growing weary.

I think faithfulness is a continual call to show up. To keep doing what you believe God has called you to do. Faithfulness is a marathon, not a sprint. But it gets discouraging when it feels like you should be at the finish line and you're actually only a mile in. I once did a 5k and practically had to be carried across the finish line. I walked 3.1 miles, but it felt like a trek across the globe. Being faithful can be discouraging if it feels like you're not making any traction.

When Jesus saw the faithful act of this widow, he called over his disciples to watch. Can you imagine God calling all the angels in heaven together to look at you? "Look, guys! No one on earth saw that, but I did."

I'm not sure if that's how it works, but it reminds me of the story of Job. He remained faithful even when he thought God had abandoned him. Little did he know, a cosmic battle between God and Satan was taking place in his backyard. All of heaven was watching to see what Job would do. Despite tragedy striking every area of his life, "Job did not sin by blaming God" (Job 1:22, NLT).

The kingdom of God is built through small acts. One day while I was working at my church's office, I got sick and vomited all over the bathroom. In the sink, on the floor, it was a mess. At that moment, the lead pastor happened to walk in. Talk about being in the wrong place at the wrong time! He took one look at the mess and said, "Oh my... let me call in the cleaning crew."

No, that's not really what he did. He cleaned everything up while making sure I was okay. He quietly cleaned up my mess when no one was watching. That's what faithfulness looked like for him at that moment.

But if you're growing weary of being faithful, the last thing you need to hear is "just keep being faithful." In these moments, we need to be reminded that God loves us even when we're *not* faithful. He's faithful when we're not. On the days we stumble, trip, and fall, we need to hear Jesus' words:

Come to me, all you who are weary and burdened, and I will give you rest. Take my yoke upon you and learn from me, for I am gentle and humble in heart, and you will find rest for your souls. For my yoke is easy and my burden is light. (Matthew 11:28–30, NIV)

Tomorrow is a new day full of new opportunities to be faithful.

Questions to Ponder:

What does the word "faithfulness" mean to you?

Is there anything you've been faithful with, but it doesn't seem to matter? How can you lean into Jesus in your times of weariness?

- Day 34 -
Open Mouth, Insert Foot

Today's Bible Reading: Mark 12:41-44

I want us to do a little thought exercise together. I know we've been studying the story of The Invisible Widow for a few days, but take a couple of minutes to read the passage again. As you read, try to imagine the scene playing out. Visualize every detail.

Did you do it? Now let me ask you a question. In your mind, what does the widow look like?

I've read this story many times throughout my life, and every time I imagine the widow as an old woman. I picture her bent over, walking with a cane, slowly making her way to the offering box. I imagine her as the old woman in front of you in line at the bank, who has a bag of 1,000 pennies she wants to deposit. She slowly opens the bag and carefully takes out each coin. *One… Two… Uh-oh, lost count! Let me start over…*

But you know what? The story never says that she's old.

The French artist James Tissot captured this scene in a painting called *The Widow's Mite.*[11] Here's his interpretation of the story on the following page:

---

11   By James Tissot — Online Collection of Brooklyn Museum; Photo: Brooklyn Museum, 2008, 00.159.211_PS2.jpg, Public Domain, https://commons.wikimedia. org/w/index.php?curid=10957531

In Tissot's depiction, the widow is relatively young, and she's caring for a child. In a time when women married young and early deaths were a common occurrence, Tissot's rendering may not be far off.

Why did I picture the widow as old? Why did you picture the widow the way you did? It's natural for us to fill in gaps to complete the story. The other day, I said every single story matters to Jesus. But getting to know a person's story takes time. And when we don't have a complete picture, we begin to fill in details to make sense of the story.

Maybe we see someone going through a hard time. Instead of having empathy and compassion, we try to explain to ourselves how they got in that mess. *Yes, his situation is sad, but he probably made a lot of poor choices to get here. He probably just didn't take his job seriously enough and got fired.* I don't think we do this because we're evil. We do it because we want to protect ourselves from sadness.

If someone is in a painful situation, I need to rationalize it somehow. If I can come up with a narrative for how that man on the street corner became homeless, maybe I'll feel a little better about passing him by. But when we make snap judgments about people, we open ourselves up to "open mouth, insert foot" moments. We say things about them that make us look foolish when the truth comes out.

One of my favorite movies is *Home Alone*. Behind all the silly slapstick humor is a profound story about how we perceive the world. At the beginning of the film, the kids tell scary stories about their neighbor, "Old Man Marley." There are rumors about him and why he's a loner.

Later in the movie, Kevin meets Marley in a church. As Kevin learns Marley's story, he realizes that they both share the same struggles. They form a friendship and encourage each other. Kevin will never see Marley the same way again.

It's not easy to learn a person's full story. It takes time and vulnerability. It's uncomfortable. But when we do, it can lead to greater understanding and deeper compassion.

🗨 Questions to Ponder:

Have you ever had an "open mouth, insert foot" moment? Has anyone ever made a snap judgment about you?

When are you most tempted to fill in details about a person's story rather than get to know the truth?

- Day 35 -
A Heart For The Broken

Today's Bible Reading: Mark 12:41-44
Supporting Passage: Matthew 5:1-12

Over the past five days, we've looked at the beautiful story of The Widow's Offering—or, as I call it, The Invisible Widow. Through her story, we learn that Jesus sees every act of faithfulness. But before we say goodbye to the widow, we need to look at the darker side of this tale. *(Dun dun duuuun!)*

A haunting question looms over this story. Why was this widow so poor? Why did she only have two copper coins to her name?

The ancient world was not very kind to widows. If a woman's husband died, she could lose all her property and financial resources. Fortunately, God set up laws to protect widows. The Pharisees were supposed to carry out these laws and help widows secure their rightful property. *Unfortunately*, these men were exploiting the system for their own gain instead.

Right before Jesus sees the widow, he points out this hypocrisy. He says:

[The Pharisees] devour widows' houses and for a show make lengthy prayers. These men will be punished most severely. (Mark 12:40, NIV)

When Jesus commends the widow for her generosity, he's also giving a stinging rebuke of the Pharisees. The Pharisees devoured her house, leaving only two small coins in their wake. Jesus recognizes that there is something wrong with this picture. He has a heart for the weak and vulnerable.

Jesus kicked off his public ministry with the Sermon on the Mount. In that first sermon, he issued a series of blessings called the Beatitudes. The people Jesus calls blessed aren't the rich and powerful. They aren't people who have it all figured out. The people he calls blessed are the people overlooked by the world.

Blessed are the poor in spirit, for theirs is the kingdom of heaven. (Matthew 5:3, NIV)

I think Jesus desperately wanted his disciples to understand this. That's why he drew attention to the widow that day. And you know what? They got it.

Mark is the shortest gospel. He got his information from the disciple Peter. And as Mark was writing, Peter must have pulled him aside and said, "Wait! Mark, I know you're trying to keep your book short, and there are so many exciting stories we can include. But there's this one story we can't leave out. It meant a lot to Jesus. So write this down..." Peter made sure The Invisible Widow would be seen and remembered by the world.

Widows have a place in God's kingdom. So do the weak, the sad, the lonely, and the brokenhearted. They are blessed because God doesn't want anyone left out.

💬 Questions to Ponder:

Are there specific groups of people your heart breaks for? How can you take one small step toward protecting them?

Read the list of blessings in Matthew 5:3–12. How would you put each one in your own words?

What is one thing you've learned about Jesus from the story of The Invisible Widow?

Encounter VIII:
Jesus Meets The Honest Criminal

When we mess up, there's nothing sweeter than receiving forgiveness. We all long for a way back home. But what happens when our time is running out, and it's impossible to set right all the things we've done wrong?

As Jesus hung on a cross in the final moments of his life, he looked over and saw another man hanging beside him. This man was brutally honest—he knew the choices he made in life led him to this fate. His pathetic story was about to end in the most humiliating way possible.

The world was done with this lifelong criminal. That meant God was done with him, too, right? He had nothing to offer now, not while being executed. Receiving forgiveness would be far too wonderful a thing to hope for.

But with Jesus, nothing is too wonderful.

* * *

You can find the story of The Honest Criminal in **Luke 23:32-43**. Take a few minutes to read it, and then we'll jump in!

- Day 36 -
An Honest Mess

Today's Bible Reading: Luke 23:32-43

Over the past few weeks, we've looked at seven encounters Jesus had with messy, broken people. If you've stayed with me this far, I want to say thank you. I appreciate you taking time out of your day to explore these stories with me. Today, we will begin looking at our final encounter. I saved this one for last because I consider it the ultimate "nobody left out" story.

It takes place on the day of Jesus' death. If there were ever a day for Jesus to not care about other people, this would be it. He's been rejected by the people he loves, beaten by soldiers, and hung on a cross to die a slow, agonizing death. And yet, he was still thinking of others first. I find that amazing. Do I have that kind of concern for people? When I get a headache, I want to curl up into a ball and shut the whole world off.

Jesus was crucified between two criminals. I wonder what these two men were thinking as they got placed next to Jesus on death row. Were they happy that at least Jesus would take the brunt of the crowd's insults? Or was it a reminder that even in their death, they would fade into the background?

One criminal mocks Jesus along with the crowd. (He gets a bad rap, but we will try to see things from his perspective in a few days.) The other criminal cries out to him:

"Jesus, remember me when you come into your kingdom." (v. 42, NIV)

This man has some audacity, doesn't he? He has lived a life of crime and is hours away from death. The clock has run out on the jumbotron, and now he's trying to make a desperate (pardon the pun) Hail Mary pass to Jesus. If I were Jesus, I would have said, *Uhhhh, I'm a little busy at the moment! Can you not see what is going on here?*

But Jesus doesn't say that. He welcomes the man. *Yes, my friend. You will not be forgotten.*

In Christian tradition, this criminal is sometimes referred to as the Good Thief. The irony, of course, is that he admitted he *wasn't* good. He was honest about his mess, and Jesus had compassion for him.

When we come to Jesus in our brokenness, he'll never turn us away. He'll never leave us out.

💬 Questions to Ponder:

What do you think it was like for the two criminals who were crucified next to Jesus?

Are you going through any situations where it feels like the clock has "run out" on you? How can you bring your mess to Jesus?

- Day 37 -
There's Always Room For Hope

Today's Bible Reading: Luke 23:32-43
Supporting Passage: Matthew 27:38-44

It must have been a strange sight for anyone who was watching.

Two men hang on crosses inches away from each other. One turns to the other and addresses him like royalty. He gasps for air between each word, suffocating under his own weight. "Jesus, remember me when you come into your kingdom."

The other man's eyes look up slowly to meet his. He spits out blood from his mouth and then replies, "Truly I tell you, today you will be with me in paradise."

If anyone in the crowd overheard this exchange, they must have laughed. Were these guys delirious from the pain? Were they hallucinating that they were in some far-off, fairy tale land? Why did the criminal think Jesus had a kingdom?

After his arrest, Jesus was mocked for being the king of the Jews. He had talked about God's kingdom a lot, and the religious leaders thought he was making a grab for earthly power. (In reality, they were the ones thirsty for power.) When Pilate sent Jesus to Herod, Herod dressed Jesus in a kingly robe and had fun ridiculing him.

The soldiers jumped on the bandwagon, too. "If you are the king of the Jews, save yourself," they yelled. Everyone mocked Jesus for being a "king"—even the two criminals he was crucified between.

In Matthew's account of this story, both criminals mock Jesus. Is this a contradiction to Luke's version? I don't think so. It took hours to die from crucifixion. As the time ticked by, the "Honest Criminal" began to see things in a new light. As Jesus grew weaker in the world's eyes, he somehow started looking more kingly to this criminal. When everyone else saw death, he saw hope. J. Ellsworth Kalas says this about the criminal's plea to Jesus:

It was a request of extraordinary faith, for if ever there was a time when Jesus did not look like an heir to a kingdom, it was at this hour. But faith always sees more than is evident to the naked eye.[12]

In Jesus' upside-down kingdom, light emerges when things seem darkest. As circumstances grow bleak, hope grows stronger. And hope says the story isn't over.

Sometimes I wish I owned a pair of Hope Goggles. I could put them on when I've hit rock bottom to see that there's still hope. They would help me see God's not done with my story.

I don't have Hope Goggles, but I do have this story to remind me that there's always room for hope.

The criminal on the cross had every reason to despair. The morning of his execution, he was dragged from his cell, kicked around, and forced to lay on two beams of wood. I can't imagine the pain as the nails were driven into his wrists. I can't imagine his fear as they raised up the cross with him attached to it. Yes, he was done for.

And then, out of nowhere, hope put him inches away from a king.

---

12   Kalas, J. Ellsworth. *The Grand Sweep: 365 Days From Genesis Through Revelation.* Nashville, TN: Abingdon, 2016.

💬 Questions to Ponder:

Why do you think the criminal started out mocking Jesus along with everyone else, but then saw him as a king?

If you had a pair of "Hope Goggles," what would you use them to see?

- Day 38 -
What Happened To The Other Criminal?

Today's Bible Reading: Luke 23:32-43 (focus on verse 39)

Over the past couple of days, we've been looking at Jesus' interaction with the criminal on the cross. In the final moments of his life, he decided to put his trust in Jesus. But there was another criminal that hung on the other side of Jesus. And this one wasn't convinced that Jesus was anything special. Even while he was experiencing the agony of crucifixion, he took the time to throw insults at Jesus:

"One of the criminals hanging beside him scoffed, "So you're the Messiah, are you? Prove it by saving yourself—and us, too, while you're at it!" (Luke 23:39, NLT)

I wonder if these two criminals knew each other. Were they friends? Did they work together, robbing travelers along the desert road? Maybe they shared their dreams of what things would be like if life had been kinder to them. Maybe they had plans to get out of the gutter one day. And then, they slipped up. They made one bad move and got caught. It was all over.

The criminal who insulted Jesus did so out of hurt and anger. His words drip with bitterness and resentment. But they ring with the same desperation as the words of the other criminal. It can be easy to dismiss this criminal as faithless. But before I do, I need to ask myself, *Have I ever lashed out at God?*

Have I ever let my disappointment with life turn into anger?

Have I ever challenged God that if he could do something to help, why doesn't he just do it?

Yes, yes, and more yes.

It's tempting to paint these two criminals as polar opposites. One commentary I read said, "The first [criminal, the one who insulted Jesus] received nothing, but the second received all that he asked."

I'm not sure I would jump to that conclusion just yet. Remember, the first criminal asked Jesus to save him. Yes, he was being sarcastic, but something inside of him hoped Jesus really did have that power.

And what was Jesus doing on that cross? He was saving the whole world. He was paying the price for that man's sins. Every act of crime he committed. Every bad decision he made. Every disappointment that made him grow bitter toward life. Even the hurtful words he was hurling at Jesus *that very moment*. Jesus was dealing with all of it.

So, what—am I saying that this criminal accepted Jesus, too? Am I trying to create a narrative that isn't there?

No. But maybe!

I'm saying we don't know. There's no way to see people's hearts, which is why we need to be careful about judging others. As we saw yesterday, both criminals started out mocking Jesus. If one had a change of heart, why couldn't the other? The last thing we know about this criminal is that he saw his friend cry out to Jesus. That means he wasn't dead yet. There was still breath in his lungs.

And as long as there's still breath in our lungs, we can cry out to Jesus, too.

💬 Questions to Ponder:

What differences do you see between the two criminals? What similarities do you see?

Have you ever lashed out at God in anger? How does it feel to know that even in those times, Jesus has paid for all your sins?

- Day 39 -
Forgiveness Culture

Today's Bible Reading: Luke 23:32-43

The criminal on the cross was not a petty thief who committed a few misdemeanors. Chances are, he had murdered some of his victims. If he was sentenced to die by crucifixion, it meant the world saw no value in him. He was beyond redemption. The point of crucifixion wasn't just to kill someone. It was to humiliate them in the process.

We may not crucify people anymore, but we still like to shame them when they make a mistake. Several years ago, the term "cancel culture" started popping up in our vocabulary. According to writer Laura Berlinsky-Schine, cancel culture "involves essentially boycotting a person because of his or her problematic behaviors or actions."[13]

Cancel culture is a complex issue, and opinions of it vary. (Just Google the term to go down the rabbit hole!) No matter your opinion of cancel culture, one thing is for sure: Our society has grown more comfortable calling out injustices. And this is a step in the right direction. Calling out racial prejudices, abuse against women, and mockery of LGBTQ+ individuals is a good thing.

But in our effort to seek justice, have we overlooked a process of redemption? We are quick to cast people out into the abyss when they mess up, but we're not quite sure how to welcome them back into the

13   Berlinsky-Schine, Laura. "We Need to Talk About the Impact of Cancel Culture." Jobs, Company Reviews, Career Advice and Community. Fairygodboss, July 8, 2019. https://fairygodboss.com/career-topics/cancel-culture.

community. Because of this, we're all terrified of making a mistake. And when we do make a mistake, we're quick to point our finger at someone who made a bigger mistake, as if to say, "*They* should be crucified, not me."

Back in Encounter IV, we met some Pharisees who were eager to start throwing stones. Maybe picking up a stone is a way to protect ourselves. It seems that as a culture, we're all racing to throw the first stone because if we don't, we may get pelted. So how do we continue to seek justice but also leave room for redemption? What's the answer?

Forgiveness.

We need to learn how to engage in forgiveness culture.

The thief on the cross was worthless in the eyes of society. He had lived a wasted life, and there was nothing he could do to make up for it. He was cast out, but Jesus offered him a path back home. It's a path that is offered to each of us, no matter how bad we've messed up.

Tomorrow, we'll take a closer look at that path.

💬 Questions to Ponder:

Have you ever seen an example where justice and redemption worked together in a positive way?

Have you ever messed up so bad that you thought you were beyond redemption? Remember that with Jesus, there's always a path back home.

- Day 40 -
The Thieves Get Heaven's Gold

Today's Bible Reading: Luke 23:32-43 (focus on verses 41-43)
Supporting Passage: Hebrews 12:1-3

For the joy set before You, You came to our rescue
And for silver You were sold, Now the thieves get heaven's gold
He who finds life will lose it, But in losing we're finding out
There's joy waiting for us — You set joy before us[14]

That verse is from one of my favorite songs, "Joy Before Us" (written by my friend Andy Simonds!). I love the phrase, *Now the thieves get heaven's gold*. It seems so unfair, and yet I smile, knowing that I will be counted among the thieves one day.

Yesterday, we saw how the criminal on the cross was cast out by society. The world saw no value in him; he was beyond redemption. There was nothing he could do to make things right—especially not now, while nailed to a cross. Despite this, Jesus still offered him forgiveness.

I want to close out our time with this criminal by taking a look at what he said while on the cross. There were four statements he made that led him down a path toward forgiveness. I think these four things will help us in times when we need to seek forgiveness from God and others.

---

14   The Quints. Joy Before Us. Selections from the Hymnody of Summit Church, Vol. 2. Andy Simonds and Greg Perkins.

1. The criminal recognized wrongdoing:

"We are punished justly." (v. 41, NIV)

The criminal acknowledged he was being punished for doing something wrong. This is a good starting point, but simply agreeing with facts isn't enough. I can rob a bank and intellectually understand why I'm being sent to jail but not have any remorse over it.

2. The criminal experienced sorrow:

"We are getting what our deeds deserve." (v. 41, NIV)

Beyond just acknowledging his sin, the criminal seemed to have sorrow over it. He was genuinely sorry for his actions.

How do you know if you're experiencing sorrow? You can take the "but" test. (Yes, you read that right. I'll explain.) If I say the word "but" during my apology, I'm probably not that sorry. (e.g., "Well, I'm sorry that you feel hurt, *but* I [insert any excuse here].") I'm still putting the blame on others and not accepting responsibility for my actions.

3. The criminal recognized that Jesus paid the cost for our sin:

"But this man has done nothing wrong." (v. 41, NIV)

The criminal may not have understood it entirely, but he knew something significant was happening on that cross. He recognized an innocent man was being punished.

I think our culture gets tripped up by this step. We realize that there is a price to pay for wrongdoing. Justice requires it. But we haven't figured out how to pay the cost, so we run around throwing stones at each other.

4. The criminal expressed a desire to move forward following Jesus:

"Jesus, remember me when you come into your kingdom." (v. 42, NIV)

I find this part the most fascinating. The criminal had mere moments to live. By all measurements, it was too late to do anything meaningful with his life. But it wasn't too late to follow Jesus. He took a step toward Jesus, and Jesus honored it. Jesus responded:

"Truly I tell you, today you will be with me in paradise." (v. 43, NIV)

I am thankful Luke included this story in his gospel. The criminal on the cross reminds me that we are never beyond redemption.

It will be a joy to be counted among the thieves.

💬 Questions to Ponder:

Is there anything you need to seek forgiveness for? Try following the four steps laid out by the criminal.

What is one thing you've learned about Jesus from the story of The Honest Criminal?

There Are More Messes Where
That Came From...

Thank you for journeying with me over the past 40 days. I hope you've enjoyed exploring these stories of Jesus loving people in their mess. If there's one thing I pray you take away from this book, it's that you are loved by Jesus right where you're at today.

We've met many characters throughout these eight stories. Each one was facing a different set of circumstances when they encountered Jesus. I want to end by asking you a question:

Was there a character you identified with the most? Why?

Whoever it was, I hope you saw Jesus' deep love for that person. And, through their story, I hope you saw Jesus' deep love for you.

You may find yourself in messy circumstances. That's okay. Wherever you find yourself, Jesus loves you.

I need that reminder every day. It's why I love to revisit these stories! And you know what? These eight encounters are only the tip of the iceberg. There are more messes where they came from! The Bible is full of stories about God loving and including messy, broken people. He invites us all to be part of his story.

Every week or so, I write an article about one of these messy Bible stories. If you'd like to receive them in your inbox, I invite you to sign up for my free digital newsletter. As a gift for subscribing, you'll get access to an extra five days of this devotional! Subscribers will also be the first to know about new book releases and other content I create. You can subscribe at NobodyLeftOut.net/9thEncounter.

But more than anything, I hope you keep reading the wonderfully messy book called the Bible. If you're unsure where to go from here, I recommend continuing to read stories about Jesus! Maybe begin by reading the Gospel of Luke ten minutes each day. Luke is my favorite gospel because it highlights Jesus' care for broken and messy people. (Three of our encounters were from that gospel.)

I'm convinced that the more we get to know Jesus, the more we'll see how loved we are by him.

It's true... He really doesn't want anyone left out!

Encounter IX:
Jesus Meets The Brave Man In The Synagogue

Ready to meet one more mess?

It wasn't easy for him to step through the synagogue doors week after week and face the silent judgment of the crowd. But the man showed up each Sabbath and tried his best not to draw attention to his hand.

Then one morning, as he enters the synagogue, he feels the stares of the religious leaders. But this time, it's more than their usual gawking; the man senses he's being used as a pawn in some kind of chess match.

He thinks about ducking out, but then Jesus walks in. After looking around for a moment, Jesus asks the man to stand next to him.

Would the man step up? And how would those religious guys react?

* * *

Subscribe to the **Nobody Left Out Newsletter**, and you'll receive this additional five-day devotional as a gift.

Get it here:
NobodyLeftOut.net/9thEncounter

A Small Favor...

Thank you so much for reading *Nobody Left Out: Jesus Meets the Messes*. This is the first devotional book I've written, and I would love to get your thoughts. It would mean a lot to me if you left an honest review on Amazon.

As you may know, Amazon reviews play an essential role in reaching other readers. They help people decide if this book is right for them. Reviews also help me gain insight into the things I got right and the areas I need to improve. I want to get better as a writer!

Based on your review, I'll continue tweaking this book's content and putting out new editions. It will also help me as I write future devotional books.

Feel free to leave a review at **NobodyLeftOut.net/BookReview**.

Thank you!

About The Author

Michael Murray is just a broken, messy guy trying to follow Jesus one step at a time. He was born with cerebral palsy, a disability that affects motor skills. Living life with CP has given Michael a unique perspective on God's grace and mercy. He created the *Nobody Left Out* book series to share the good news that every single person matters to Jesus.

Michael and his wife Diana live in Orlando, Florida, with their son Emmett and dog Ruby. (Diana is an amazing artist!) He attends Summit Church, where he serves as a writer and actor on the family productions team. Michael is a big fan of sweet tea, musicals, and writing about himself in the third person.

Connect with Michael:

Website: NobodyLeftOut.net
YouTube Channel: YouTube.com/MichaelMurrayIsMessy
Facebook: Facebook.com/NobodyLeftOut
Instagram: Instagram.com/MichaelJMurray83

Made in the USA
Las Vegas, NV
10 October 2021